A-Z SOUTHAMPTON

REFERENCE

Motorway	**M27**	Airport	✈
A Road	**A33**	Berth Number	102
B Road	**B3033**	Car Park (selected)	Ⓟ
Dual Carriageway		Church or Chapel	†
One-way Street		Cycleway (selected)	🚲
Traffic flow on A Roads is also indicated by a heavy line on the driver's left.		Dock Gate Number	⑤
Road Under Construction		Fire Station	■
Opening dates are correct at the time of publication.		Hospital	Ⓗ
Proposed Road		House Numbers (A & B Roads only)	37 44
Restricted Access		Information Centre	🅸
Pedestrianized Road		National Grid Reference	⁴45
Track / Footpath		Police Station	▲
Residential Walkway		Post Office	★
Railway	Station / Level Crossing / Tunnel	Toilet	▽
Built-up Area	MILL RD.	Educational Establishment	▢
Local Authority Boundary		Hospital or Healthcare Building	▢
National Park Boundary		Industrial Building	▢
Postcode Boundary		Leisure or Recreational Facility	▢
		Place of Interest	▢
		Public Building	▢
Map Continuation	40 / Large Scale City Centre 4	Shopping Centre or Market	▢
		Other Selected Buildings	▢

SCALE

Large Scale Pages 4-5   1:7,920

0	⅛	¼ Mile
0	100	200	300 Metres

8 inches (20.32cm) to 1 mile   12.63cm to 1km

T0328029

EDITION 9   2021

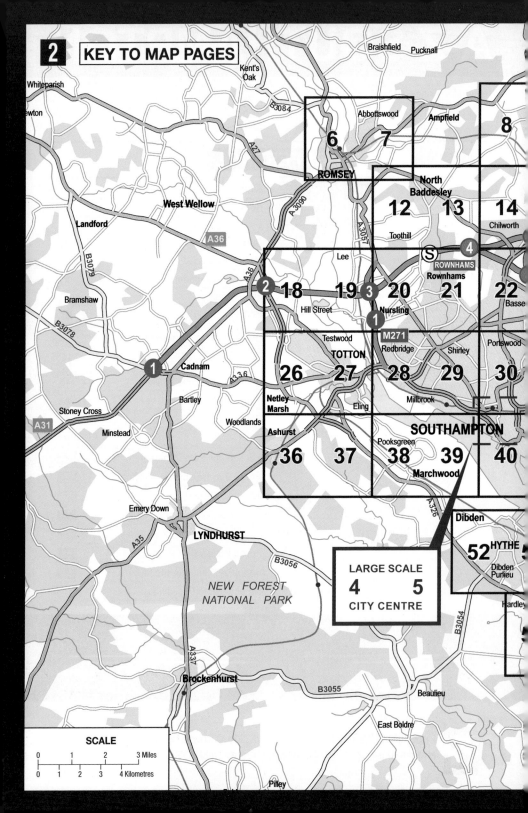

KEY TO MAP PAGES

2

Braishfield Pucknall

Kent's
Oak

Whiteparish

ewton

B3084

Abbottswood

Ampfield

8

6

7

ROMSEY

North
Baddesley

12 **13** **14**

West Wellow

A3090

Toothill

Chilworth

Landford

A36

A3057

Lee

S
ROWNHAMS **4**

B3079

Rownhams

Bramshaw

2 **18** **19** **3** **20** **21** **22**

Hill Street

Nursling

Basse

B3078

1

Testwood

M271

Redbridge

Shirley

Portswood

Cadnam

TOTTON

26 **27** **28** **29** **30**

A336

1

Bartley

Netley
Marsh

Eling

Millbrook

Stoney Cross

A31

Woodlands

Ashurst

SOUTHAMPTON

Minstead

36 **37** **38** **39** **40**

Pooksgreen

Marchwood

Emery Down

A326

Dibden

LYNDHURST

B3056

52 HYTHE

NEW FOREST
NATIONAL PARK

LARGE SCALE
4   **5**
CITY CENTRE

Dibden
Purlieu

A337

B3054

Hardley

Brockenhurst

B3055

Beaulieu

East Boldre

SCALE

0   1   2   3 Miles

0   1   2   3   4 Kilometres

Pilley

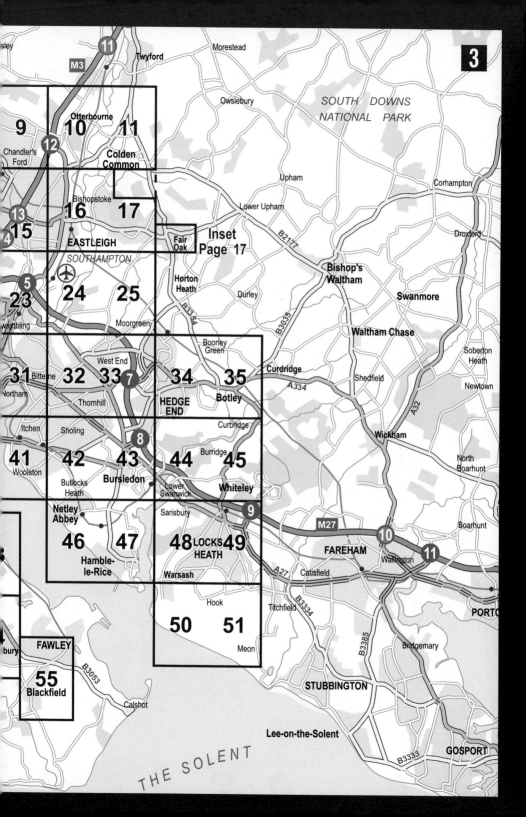

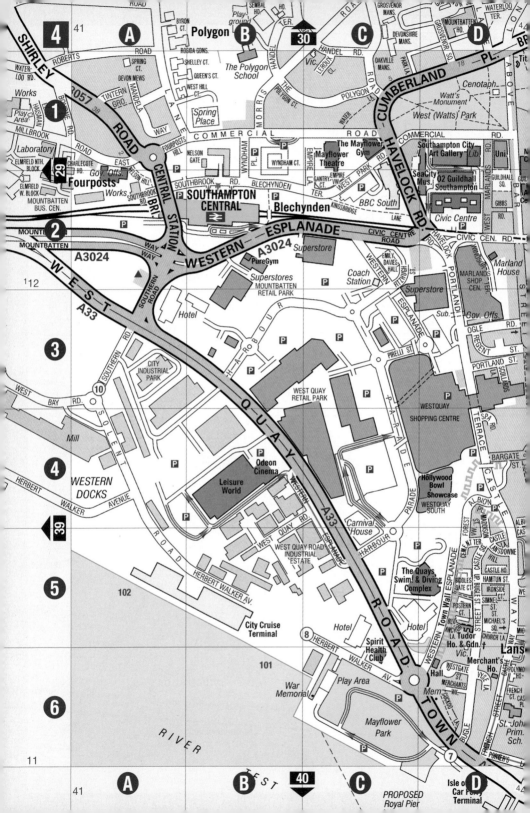

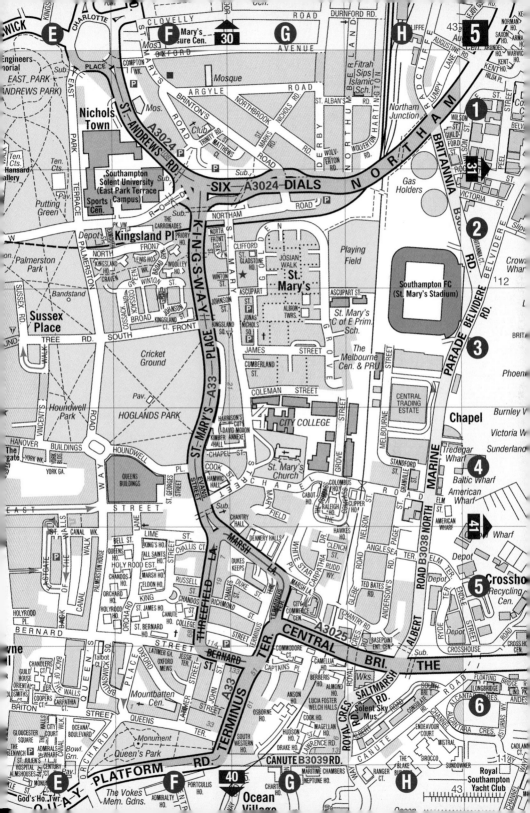

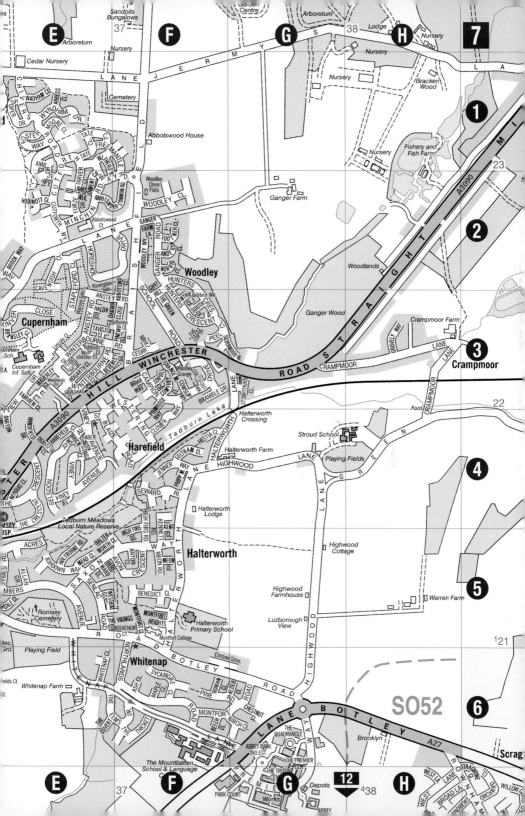

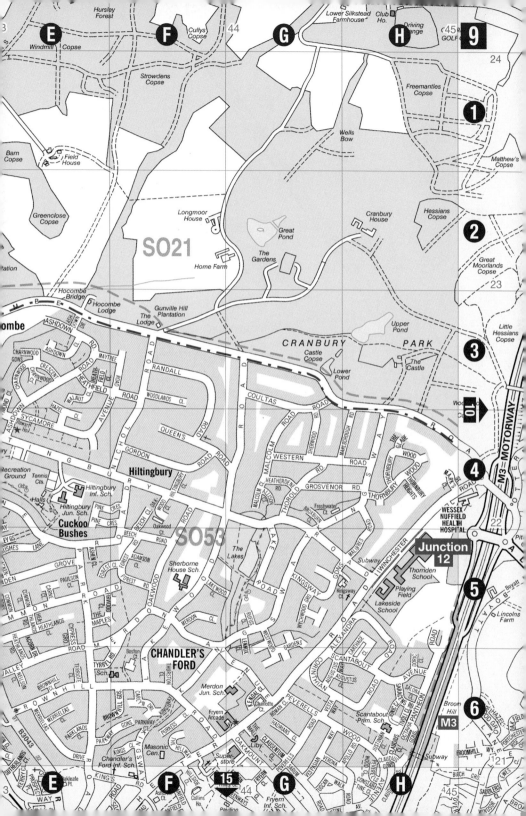

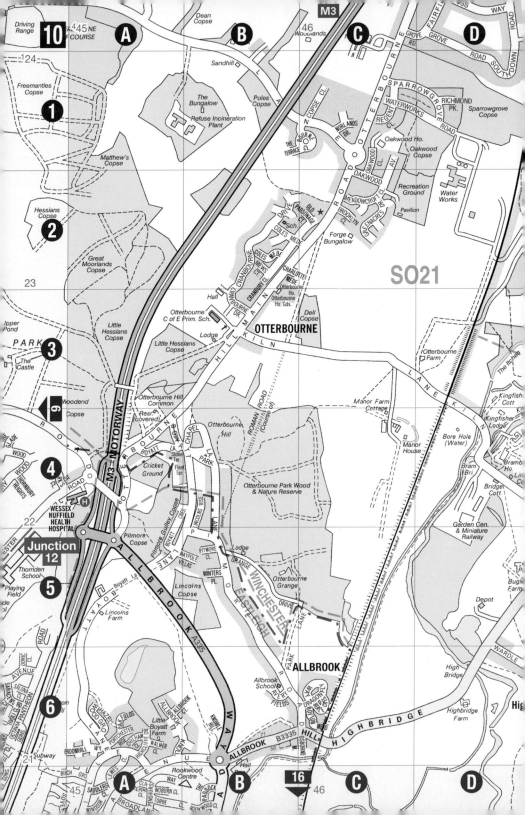

E **F** **G** **H** **11**

SOUTH DOWNS NATIONAL PARK

1
2
3
4
5
6

Recreation Ground
Colleton House
Gabriels Farm
Knighton
Keeper Cottag

MANOR FARM GRN.
Manor Farm
Toll Gate Cottage

HARE
LANE

HIGH

B3335
ROAD

MAIN

B3335 ROAD
B3354

Twyford Moors House

WOODLAND

DROVE

Park Farm

The Dell
Colden Covert

Taylor's Copse

Colden Common Park

PARK COPSE
Hound Ro

Rosemary Lea
RIVER ITCHEN
Stubbington Copse

FLEMING PL.
COLVEDENE
Fernhurst
ORCHARD CL.
NEW
ROAD

Pav.
Recreation Ground

FRANCIS COPSE
BOYES CL.

LANE
BOYES

Nordeg

Tanglewood Equestrian Centre

P

East Lodge

MOORS

LOWER

BRAMPTON
CHESTNUT
SPRINGFIELD AV.

HUNTS CL.

ROAD

LANE

Chalk Dell Copse

King's Copse

BRAMBRIDGE PARK

The Avenue

SUNNINGDALE MOBILE HOME PK.
SPRING

Fountain
SPRING CL.
HOUSE CL.
HILL
HAZEL CLOSE

Clayfield

The Manor House

Sandyfields Nurseries

Stratton's Copse
Bear's Copse
Inley's Copse

LANE

HIGHBRIDGE

Comm. Cen.
Colden Common Prim. Sch.

VIGOR
BROADLAND

COLDEN COMMON

AVONDALE MOBILE HOME PK.

GLEN PARK MOBILE HOME PARK.

BLACKNELL'S Copse

Brambridge

ROAD

MOORS
ROAD
UPPER

OAK TREE CL.
PENNINGTON CL.
FARM CL.
BURR CL.
BRICKMAKERS CL.
SETTERS CL.
PALLEY
THINKING GRN.

WHITEBEAM
WAY

ST.

VIGOR

SASO
WESSEX W.
BLACKTHORN
WILLOW
NIGUMA

ROAD

MAIN

B3354

Trinity Ct.

ROAD

B3335

CHURCH

GRAYS CL.
PIPING CL.
PIPING ROAD
LEES VALLEY CL.

FEWINS DR.
SKITTLE GRN.
HOLLY LA.
VEAR'S LA.

HAWTHORN
VEAR'S
ELDER GRN.
FINCHES
BRAMBLES CL.

Colden Common Wood

Mallard Point

SO50

Brambridge Lodge

Hillside Cott.

HACK

NOB'S

LANE

SO50

Woodcroft Lodge

Hill's Farm House

Upper Brambridge Farm

Nob's Crook

CROOK

B3354

Fisher's Pond Wood

Leylands Farm

Fisher's Pond

PORT

Fisher's Pond

121

E **17** **F** **G** **H**

Bushyclose Plantation
IDEAL PARK HOMES CARAVAN SITE
ROWLEY GREEN RD.

48

449
B2177

7

48

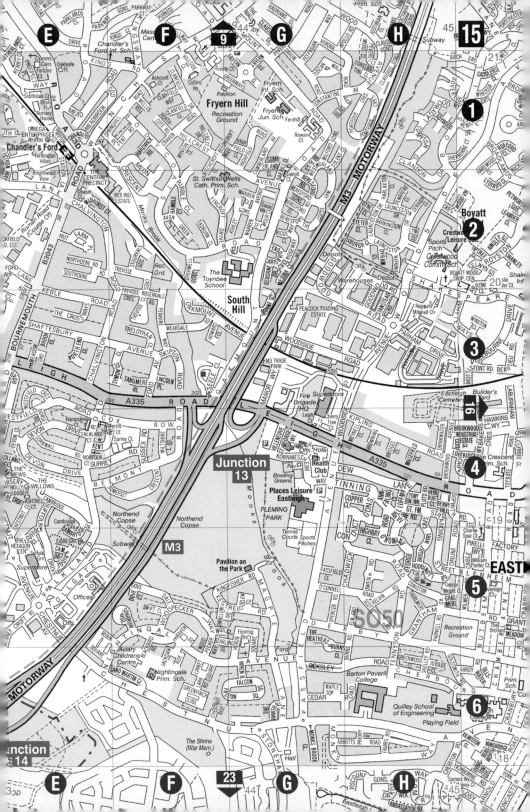

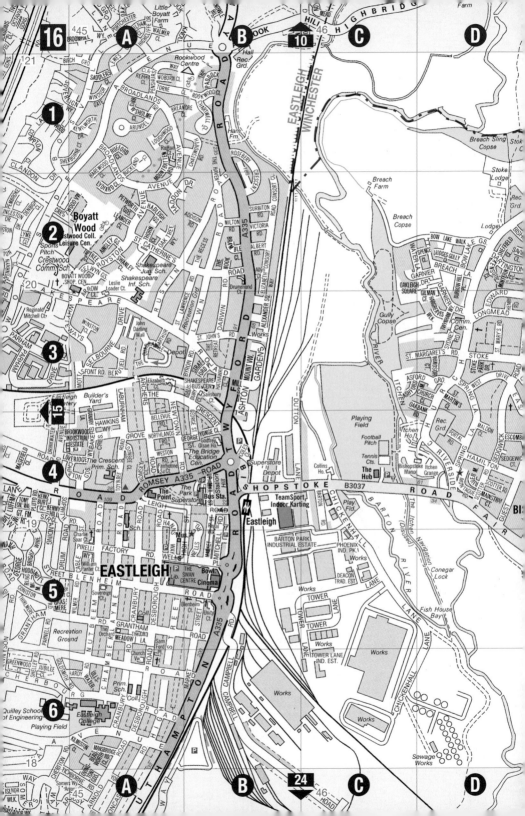

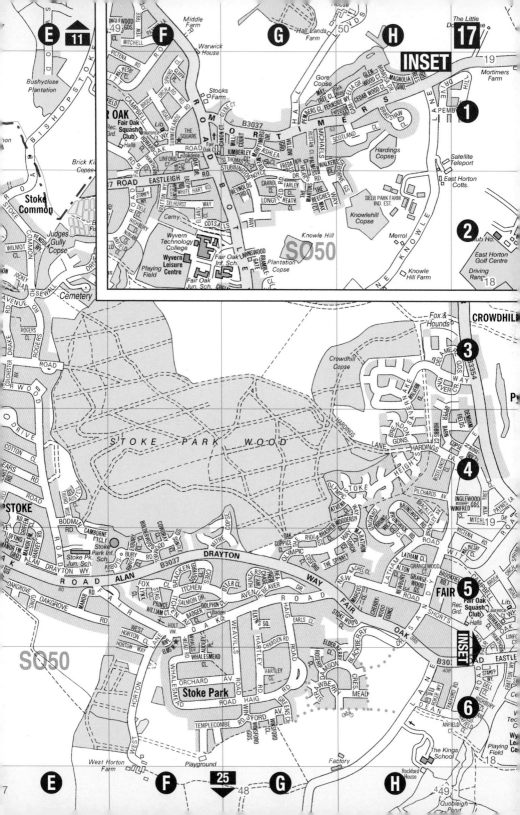

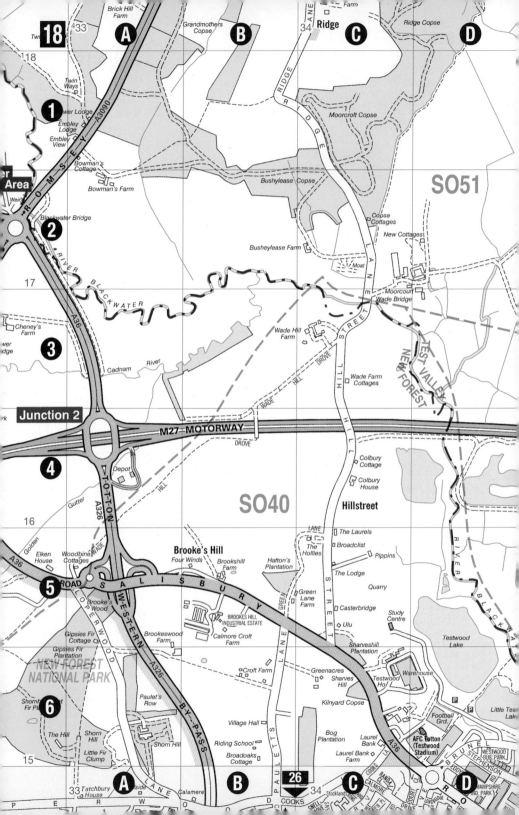

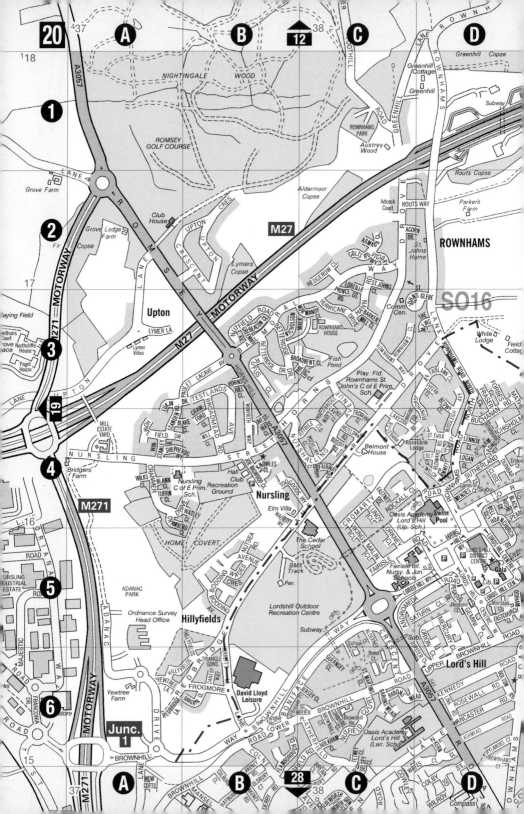

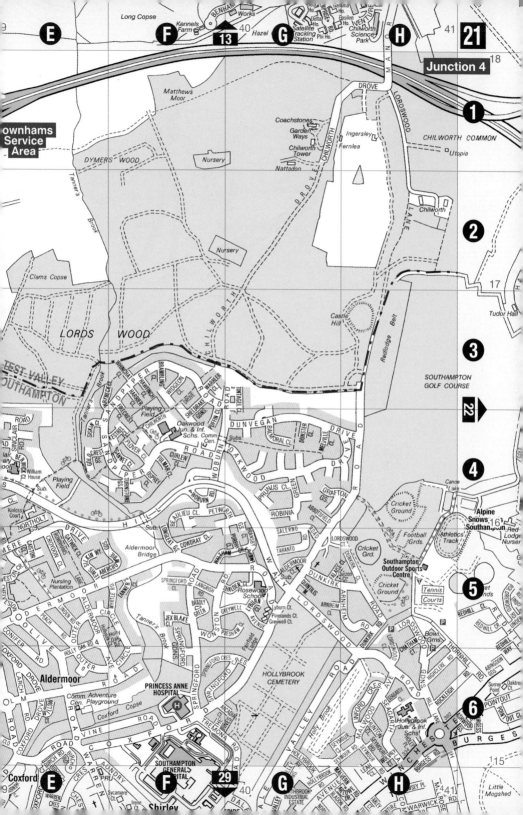

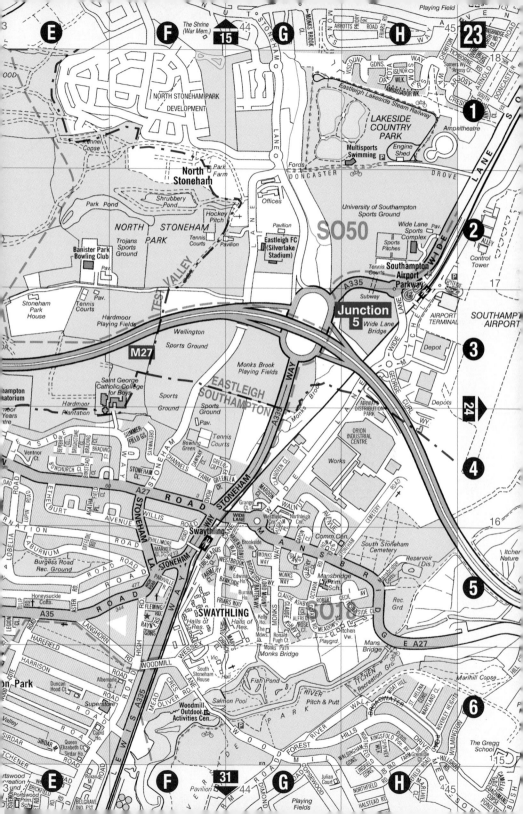

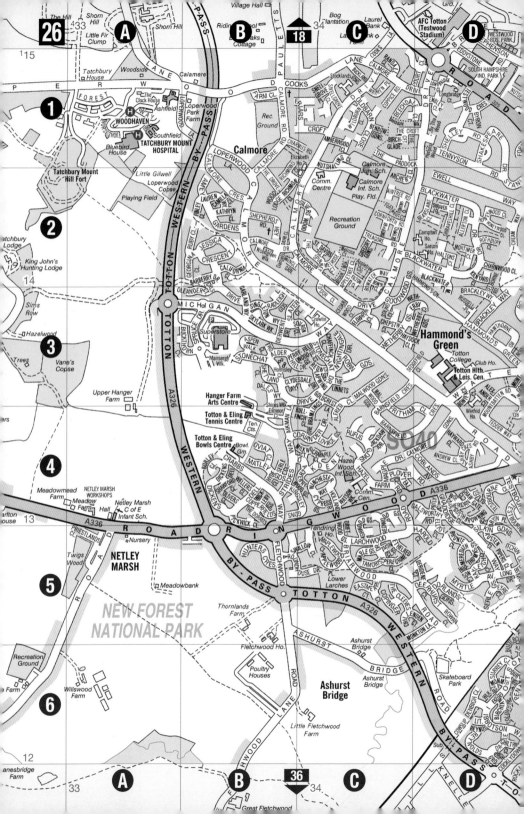

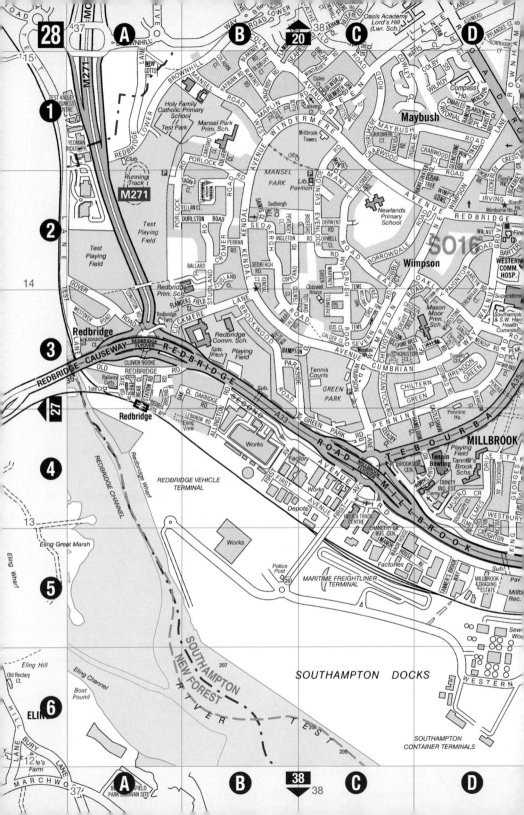

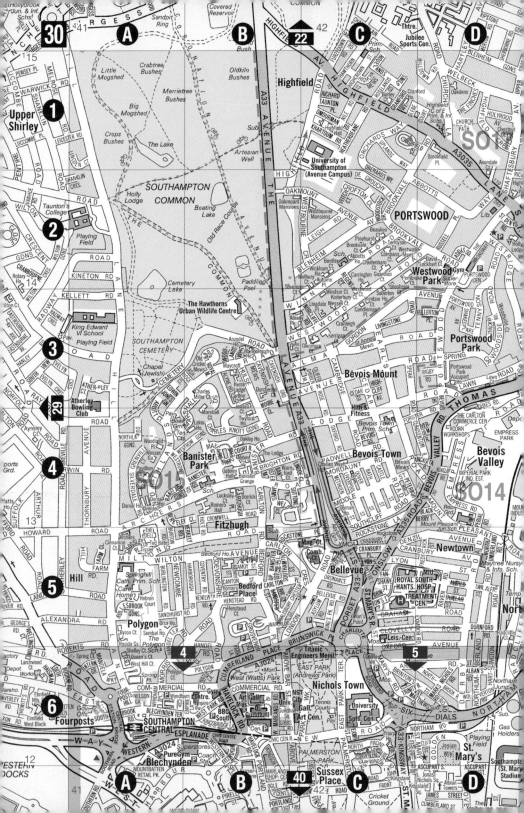

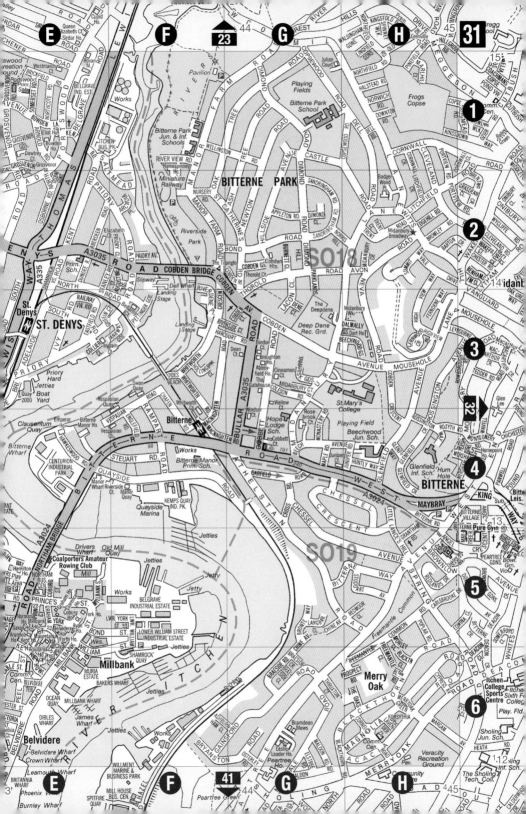

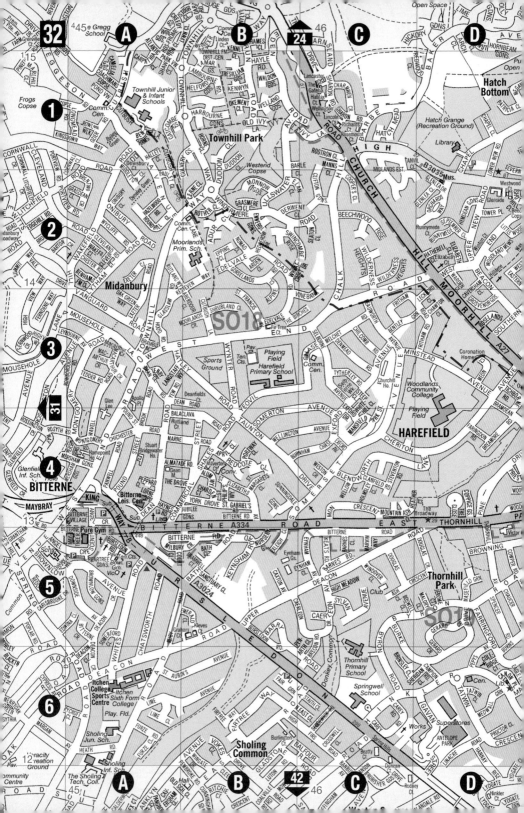

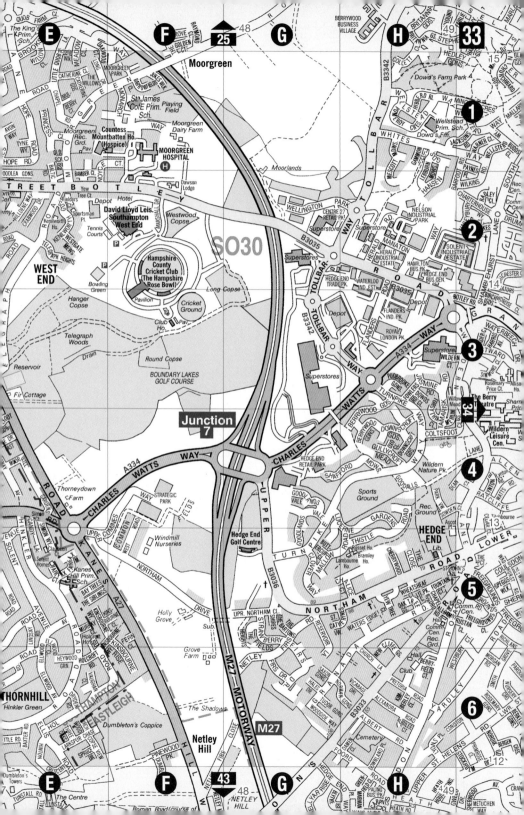

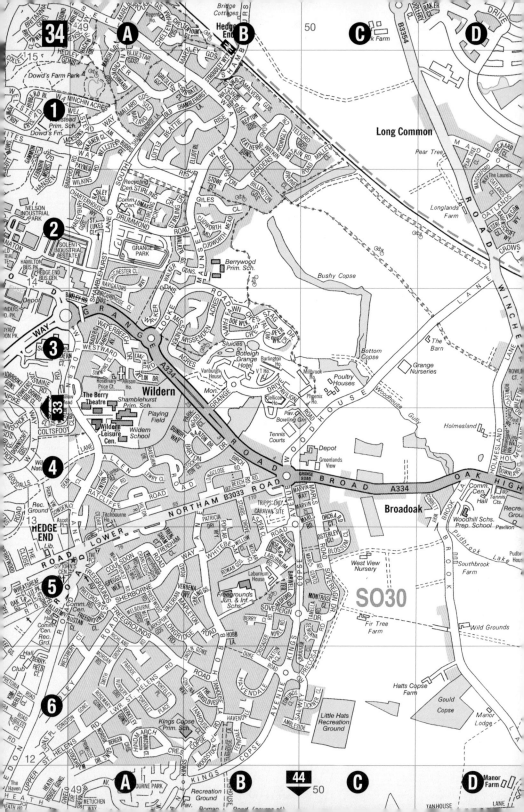

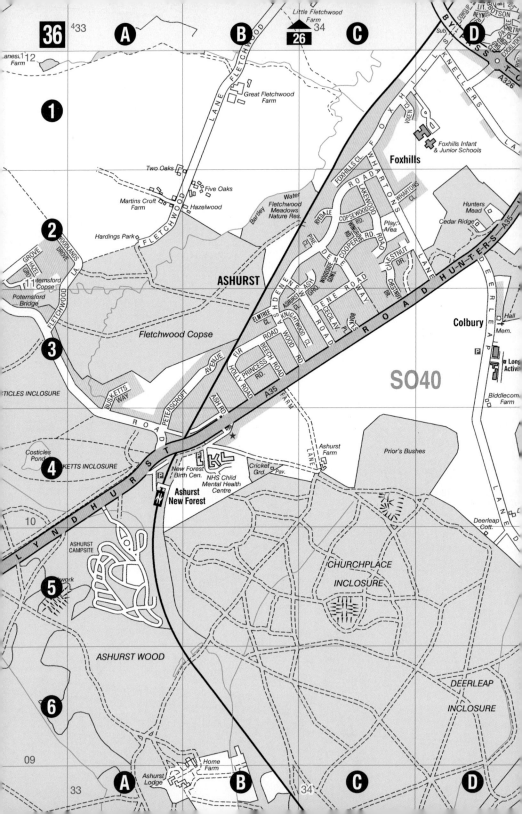

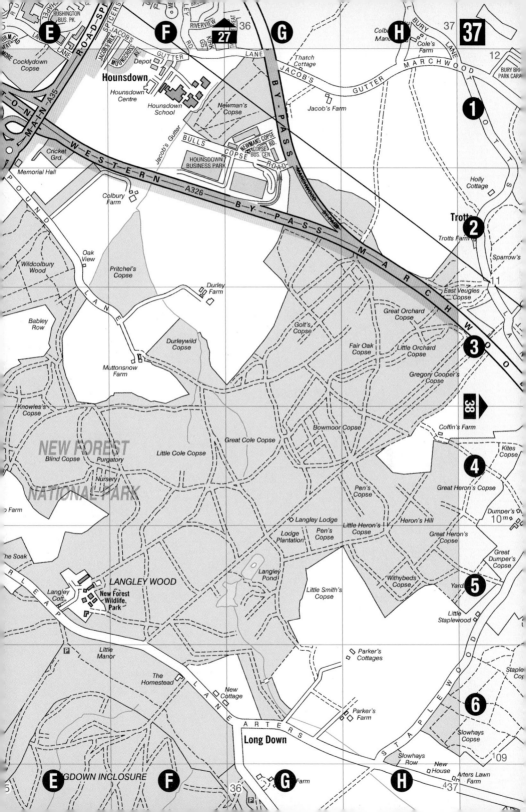

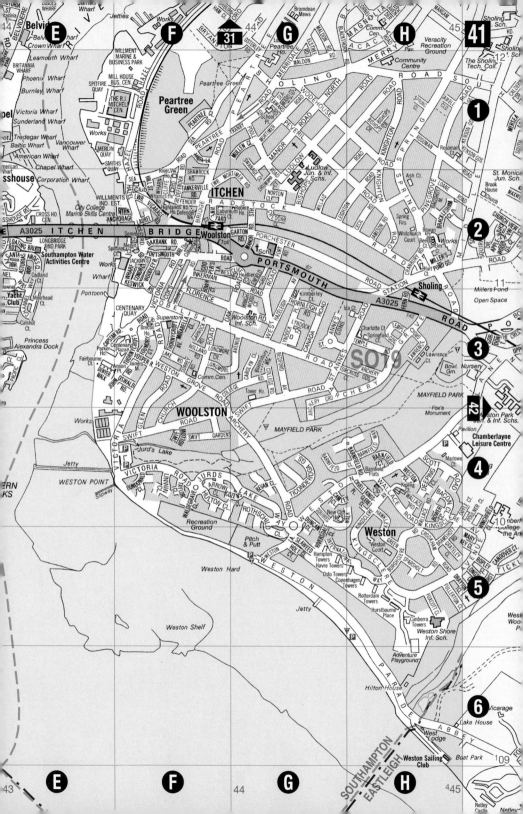

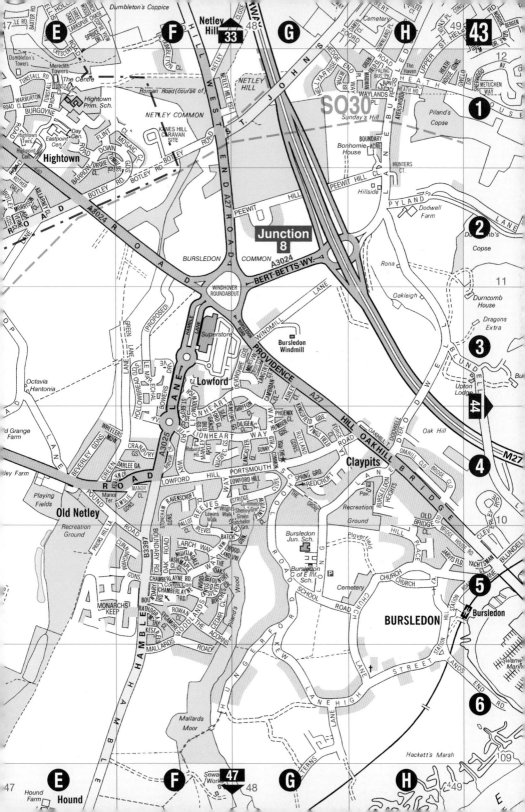

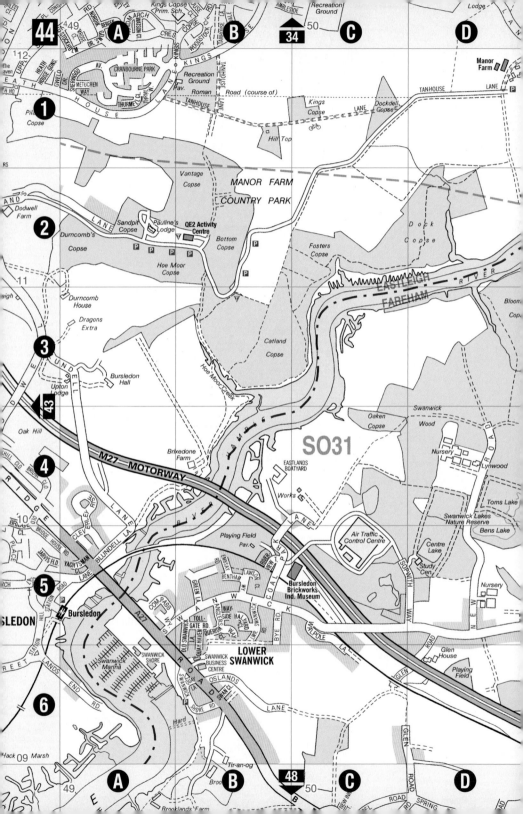

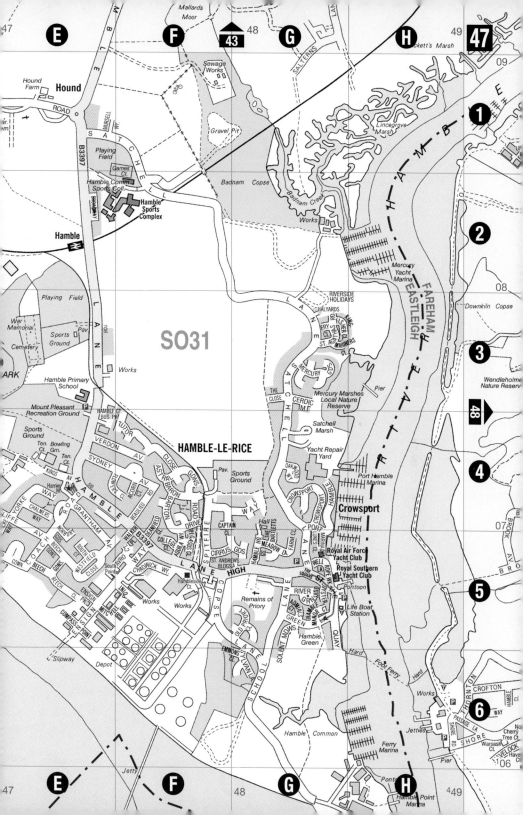

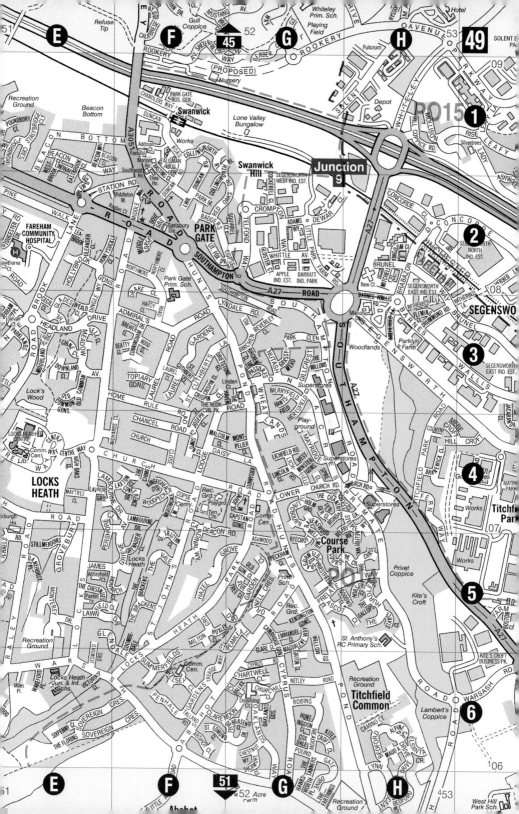

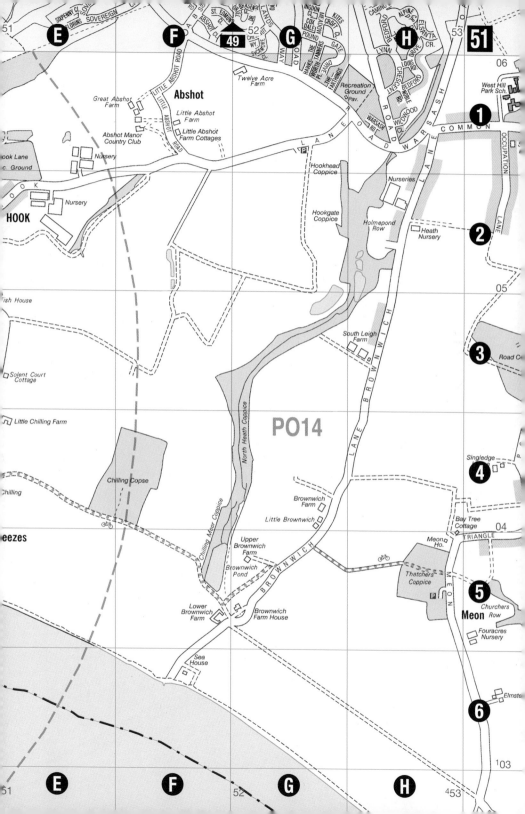

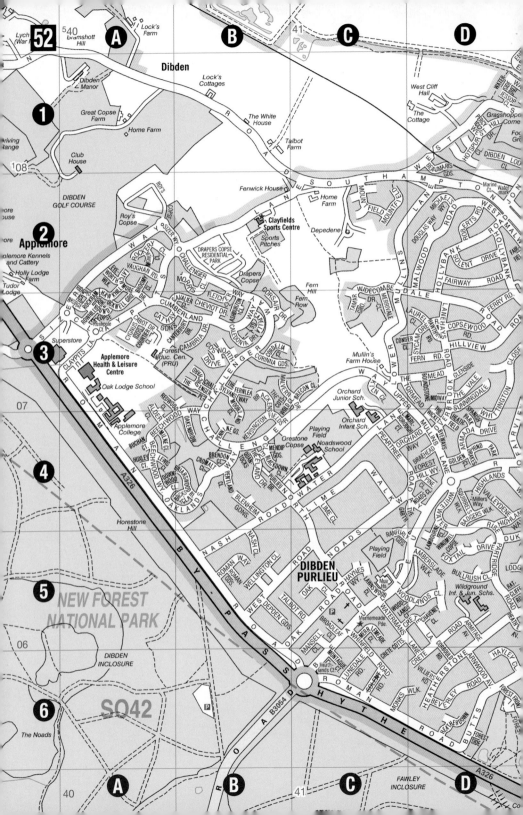

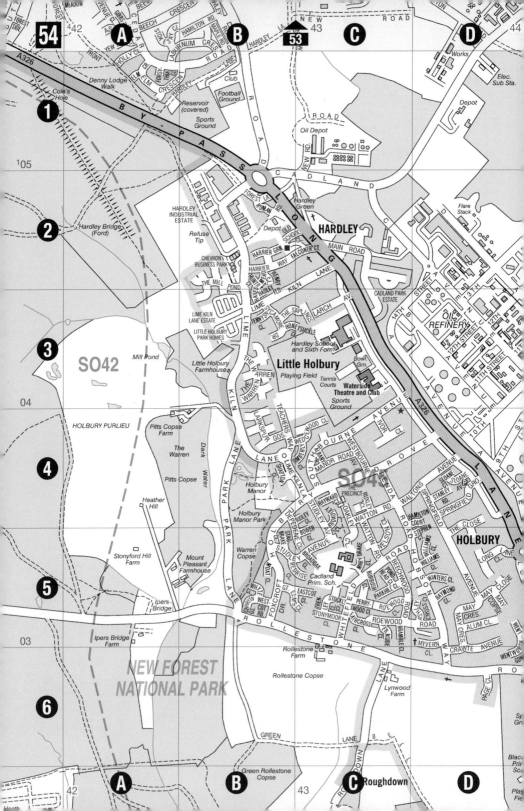

INDEX

Including Streets, Places & Areas, Hospitals etc., Industrial Estates,
Selected Flats & Walkways, Service Areas, Stations and Selected Places of Interest.

HOW TO USE THIS INDEX

1. Each street name is followed by its Postcode District, then by its Locality abbreviation(s) and then by its map reference; e.g. **Agitator Rd.** S045: F'ley..........1H **55** is in the S045 Postcode District and the Fawley Locality and is to be found in square 1H on page **55**. The page number is shown in bold type.

2. A strict alphabetical order is followed in which Av., Rd., St., etc. (though abbreviated) are read in full and as part of the street name; e.g. **Broad La.** appears after **Broadlands Rd.** but before **Broadleaf Cl.**

3. Streets and a selection of flats and walkways that cannot be shown on the mapping, appear in the index with the thoroughfare to which they are connected shown in brackets; e.g. **Abbey Wlk.** S051: Rom..........5A **6** (off Church St.)

4. Addresses that are in more than one part are referred to as not continuous.

5. Places and areas are shown in the index in BLUE TYPE and the map reference is to the actual map square in which the town centre or area is located and not to the place name shown on the map; e.g. ABBOTSWOOD..........1E **7**

6. An example of a selected place of interest is **Berry Theatre, The**..........4A **34**

7. An example of a station is Ashurst New Forest Station (Rail)..........4A **36**

8. An example of a junction name or service area is ROWNHAMS SERVICE AREA..........1D **20**

9. An example of a Hospital, Hospice or selected Healthcare facility is FAREHAM COMMUNITY HOSPITAL..........2E **49**

10. Map references for entries that appear on large scale page **4** & **5** are shown first, with small scale map references shown in brackets; e.g. **Albert Rd Nth.** S014: South..........5H **5** (2D **40**)

GENERAL ABBREVIATIONS

App. : Approach	**Dr.** : Drive	**La.** : Lane	**Rdbt.** : Roundabout
Arc. : Arcade	**E.** : East	**Lit.** : Little	**Shop.** : Shopping
Av. : Avenue	**Ent.** : Enterprise	**Lwr.** : Lower	**Sth.** : South
Blvd. : Boulevard	**Est.** : Estate	**Mnr.** : Manor	**Sq.** : Square
Bri. : Bridge	**Fld.** : Field	**Mkt.** : Market	**St.** : Street
Bldgs. : Buildings	**Flds.** : Fields	**Mdw.** : Meadow	**Ter.** : Terrace
Bus. : Business	**Gdn.** : Garden	**Mdws.** : Meadows	**Trad.** : Trading
Cvn. : Caravan	**Gdns.** : Gardens	**M.** : Mews	**Up.** : Upper
Cen. : Centre	**Gth.** : Garth	**Mt.** : Mount	**Vw.** : View
Circ. : Circle	**Ga.** : Gate	**Mus.** : Museum	**Vs.** : Villas
Cl. : Close	**Gt.** : Great	**Nth.** : North	**Vis.** : Visitors
Cnr. : Corner	**Grn.** : Green	**Pde.** : Parade	**Wlk.** : Walk
Cott. : Cottage	**Gro.** : Grove	**Pk.** : Park	**W.** : West
Cotts. : Cottages	**Hgts.** : Heights	**Pas.** : Passage	**Yd.** : Yard
Ct. : Court	**Ho.** : House	**Pl.** : Place	
Cres. : Crescent	**Ind.** : Industrial	**Ri.** : Rise	
Cft. : Croft	**Info.** : Information	**Rd.** : Road	

LOCALITY ABBREVIATIONS

Abshot: P014...........Abs	**Compton**: S021...........Comp	**Hursley**: S021...........Hurs	**Sarisbury Green**: S031...........Sar G
Ampfield: S051...........Ampf	**Crampmoor**: S051...........Cram	**Hythe**: S045...........Hythe	**Segensworth**: P015...........Seg
Ashurst: S040...........A'hst	**Curdridge**: S030, S032...........Curd	**Lepe**: S045...........Lepe	**Shawford**: S021...........Shaw
Bassett: S016, S017...........Bass	**Dibden Purlieu**: S045...........Dib P	**Locks Heath**: S031...........Loc H	**Southampton Airport**: S018...........S'ton A
Bishop's Waltham: S032...........Bis W	**Dibden**: S045...........Dib	**Lower Swanwick**: S031...........Lwr Swan	**Southampton**: S014, S015,
Bishopstoke: S050...........B'stke	**Eastleigh**: S050...........E'leigh	**Marchwood**: S040...........March	S016, S017, S018, S019...........South
Blackfield: S045...........Blac	**Eling**: S040...........Elin	**Netley Abbey**: S031...........Net A	**Swanwick**: S031...........Swanw
Botley: S030, S032...........Botl	**Fair Oak**: S050...........Fair O	**Netley Marsh**: S040...........Net M	**Swaythling**: S016, S017, S018...........S'ing
Braishfield: S051...........Brai	**Fawley**: S045...........F'ley	**North Baddesley**: S052...........N Bad	**Titchfield Common**: P014, S031...........Titch C
Brambridge: S050...........B'dge	**Hamble-le-Rice**: S031...........Hamb	**Nursling**: S016...........Nur	**Titchfield**: P014, P015...........Titch
Burridge: S031...........Burr	**Hardley**: S045...........Hard	**Old Netley**: S031...........Old N	**Toothill**: S051...........Toot
Bursledon: S031...........Burs	**Hedge End**: S030, S032...........Hed E	**Otterbourne**: S021...........Ott	**Totton**: S040...........Tott
Calmore: S040...........Calm	**Highbridge**: S050...........Highb	**Ower**: S051...........Ower	**Twyford**: S021...........Twy
Chandler's Ford: S052, S053...........Cha F	**Holbury**: S045...........Holb	**Park Gate**: S031...........P Ga	**Warsash**: S031...........Wars
Chilworth: S016...........Chil	**Horton Heath**: S050...........Hor H	**Romsey**: S051...........Rom	**West End**: S018, S030...........W End
Colden Common: S021...........Col C	**Hound**: S031...........Hou	**Rownhams**: S016...........Rown	**Whiteley**: P015...........White

---

1

1st St. S045: F'ley.............. 2G **55**	**Abbey, The** S051: Rom..................5A **6**	**Abercrombie Gdns.**
2nd St. S045: F'ley..............2F **55**	**Abbey Cl.** S045: Hythe................3E **53**	S016: South.....................5E **21**
3d Health & Fitness 2D **14**	**Abbey Ct.** S015: South 4B **30**	**Aberdeen Rd.** S017: South..........2E **31**
3rd St. S045: F'ley..............2F **55**	**Abbey Ent. Cen.** S051: Rom.......2B **12**	**Aberdour Cl.** S018: South.............3B **32**
4th St. S045: F'ley..............2F **55**	**Abbeyfield Ct.** S031: Loc H.........5E **49**	**Abingdon Gdns.** S016: Bass........6A **22**
.... (not continuous)	**Abbeyfield Ho.** S018: South 3G **31**	**Above Bar St.**
5th St. S045: F'ley..............2E **55**	**Abbeyfields Cl.** S031: Net A........1C **46**	S014: South...............±...1D **4** (6B **30**)
.... (not continuous)	**Abbey Fruit Pk. Ind. Est.**	.... (not continuous)
6th St. S045: F'ley..............1E **55**	S031: Net A..................6B **42**	**Abraham Cl.** S030: Botl...............6C **34**
.... (not continuous)	**Abbey Hill** S031: Net A................5H **41**	**ABSHOT** 1F **51**
7th St. S045: F'ley..............2E **55**	**Abbey M.** S031: Net A..................1A **46**	**Abshot Cl.** P014: Titch C 6F **49**
.... (not continuous)	**Abbey Pk. Ind. Est.** S051: Rom 6G **7**	**Abshot Rd.** P014: Titch C............6F **49**
8th St. S045: F'ley..............1E **55**	**Abbey Wlk.** S051: Rom................5A **6**	**Acacia Rd.** S019: South 6H **31**
12th St. S045: F'ley..............3C **54**	....................(off Church St.)	**Acanthus Cl.** P015: White...........4H **45**
.... (not continuous)	**Abbey Water** S051: Rom.............5A **6**	**Acastra Ho.** S019: South..............3F **41**
13th St. S045: F'ley..............3C **54**	**Abbotsbury Rd.** S050: B'stke......5E **17**	....................(off John Thornycroft Rd.)
14th St. S045: F'ley..............3C **54**	**Abbotsfield** S040: Tott................4E **27**	**Acorn Cl.** S040: March................4E **39**
	Abbotsfield Cl. S016: South.......4G **21**	**Acorn Cl.** S031: Hamb................4F **47**
	Abbots Way S031: Net A.............1C **46**	**Acorn Dr.** S016: Rown................2C **20**
	ABBOTSWOOD 1E **7**	**Acorn Dr.** S053: Cha F 6E **9**
	Abbotswood Cl. S051: Rom.........3F **7**	**Acorn Gro.** S053: Cha F 3B **14**
	Abbotswood Comn. Rd.	**Acorn Ind. Est.** S016: South 1F **29**
	S051: Rom...........................2E **7**	**Acorns, The** S031: Burs..............5F **43**
	Abbotswood Ct. S051: Rom.........2E **7**	**Acorn Workshops** S014: South... 4D **30**
	Abbotts Ho. S017: South.............2C **30**	**Adams Cl.** S030: Hed E...............6H **25**
	Abbotts Rd. S050: E'leigh...........6G **15**	**Adamson Cl.** S053: Cha F............5F **9**
	Abbotts Way S017: South 2D **30**	**Adams Rd.** S045: Hythe..............4E **53**

A

Aaron Cl. S040: March.............. 3D **38**		
A Av. S045: F'ley.............3C **54**		
.... (not continuous)		
Abbess Cl. S051: Rom 1E **7**		

Adams Way P015: Seg................ 2G **49**	
Adams Wood Dr.	
S040: March 4D **38**	
Adanac Dr. S016: Nur 5A **20**	
Adanac Pk. S016: Nur................5A **20**	
Adcock Ct. S016: Rown..............2C **20**	
Addison Cl. S051: Rom 3E **7**	
Addison Cl. S031: P Ga................1F **49**	
Addison Rd. S031: Sar G 1D **48**	
Addison Rd. S050: E'leigh...........2B **16**	
Addis Sq. S017: South 2D **30**	
.... (not continuous)	
Adelaide Rd. S017: South............3E **31**	
Adela Verne Cl. S019: South.......2E **43**	
Adey Cl. S019: South...................3B **42**	
Admirals Cl. S045: F'ley..............2H **55**	
Admiral's Rd. S031: Loc H...........3F **49**	
Admirals Way S045: Hythe...........2E **53**	
Admirals Wharf	
S014: South 6E **5** (2C **40**)	
....................(off Lwr. Canal Wlk.)	
Admiralty Ho.	
S014: South 6F **5** (3C **40**)	
Admiralty Way S040: March 2D **38**	
Adur Cl. S018: W End..................2B **32**	
Africa Dr. S040: March................ 4D **38**	

Agincourt Dr. – Badgers Run

Agincourt Dr. SO31: Sar G........... 2D 48
.... (not continuous)
Agitator Rd. SO45: F'ley............... 1H 55
Agwi Rd. SO45: F'ley................. 1H 55
Aikman La. SO40: Tott 4B 26
Ailsa La. SO19: South...................1F 41
Ainsley Gdns. SO50: E'leigh 2A 16
Aintree Ct. PO15: White............... 5G 45
Aintree Rd. SO40: Calm................2C 26
Airways Distribution Pk.
SO18: S'ing............................... 3H 23
Alan Chun Ho. SO31: Net A 6C 42
Alandale Rd. SO19: South 1D 42
Alan Drayton Way SO50: B'stke...5E 17
.... (not continuous)
Albacore Av. SO31: Wars.............6C 48
Albany Pk. Ct. SO17: South..........3B 30
Albany Rd. SO15: South 5G 29
Albany Rd. SO45: Holb 4B 54
Albany Rd. SO51: Rom...................5B 6
Albemarle Ct. SO17: South..........6E 23
Albert Cl. SO31: Net A 2B 46
.... (not continuous)
Albert Rd. SO30: Hed E 6H 33
Albert Rd. SO50: E'leigh 2B 16
Albert Rd. Nth.
SO14: South......................5H 5 (2D 40)
Albert Rd. Sth.
SO14: South......................6H 5 (2D 40)
Albion Pl. SO14: South 4D 4 (1B 40)
.... (not continuous)
Albion Towers
SO14: South......................3G 5 (1D 40)
Albury Pl. SO53: Cha F..................5C 8
Alcantara Cres.
SO14: South...................... 6H 5 (2E 41)
Alder Cl. SO21: Col C.................. 5G 11
Alder Cl. SO40: March 3D 38
Alder Cl. SO45: Dib P..................4A 52
Alder Cl. SO51: Rom.................... 6G 7
Alder Hill Dr. SO40: Tott 3B 26
ALDERMOOR.................................6D 20
Aldermoor Av. SO16: South...........5E 21
Aldermoor Cl. SO16: South 5G 21
Aldermoor Rd. SO16: South 5E 21
Alderney Cl. SO16: South 5C 20
Alder Rd. SO16: South................. 5D 20
Alderwood Av. SO53: Cha F 1C 14
Alexander Ct. SO15: South........... 5H 29
Alexander Sq. SO50: E'leigh..........3B 16
Alexandra Cl. SO45: Hythe 2E 53
Alexandra Rd. SO15: South.......... 5H 29
Alexandra Rd. SO30: Hed E.......... 6H 33
Alexandra Rd. SO45: Hythe 2E 53
Alexandra Rd. SO53: Cha F........... 6G 9
Alexandra Way SO30: Botl 4E 35
Alfred Cl. SO40: Tott.....................4B 26
Alfred Rose Ct. SO18: S'ing 5G 23
Alfred St. SO14: South.................. 5D 30
Alfriston Gdns. SO19: South 1B 42
Allan Gro. SO51: Rom.....................5E 7
ALLBROOK.....................................6B 10
Allbrook Knoll SO50: E'leigh 6A 10
Allbrook Way SO50: E'leigh...........5A 10
Allen Rd. SO30: Hed E...................4A 34
Allerton Cl. SO40: Tott..................2C 26
Allington La. SO30: W End 6B 24
Allington La. SO50: Fair O 2G 25
Allington Mnr. Farm Bus. Cen.
SO50: Fair O...............................2E 25
Allington Rd. SO15: South............4B 28
Allison Ho. SO30: Hed E 4A 34
Allotment Rd. SO30: Hed E 5H 33
Allotment Rd. SO31: Sar G...........2C 48
All Saints Cl. SO16: South 2B 28
All Saints Ho.
SO14: South..................... 5F 5 (2C 40)
............................(off Orchard La.)
Allyn Ct. SO50: E'leigh..................2B 16
Alma Rd. SO14: South 3C 30
Alma Rd. SO51: Rom.......................5B 6
Almatade Rd. SO18: South............4A 32
Almond Ct. SO15: South............... 5G 29
Almond Ho. SO14: South ...6G 5 (2D 40)
.... (off Royal Cres. Rd.)
Almond Rd. SO15: South.............. 5G 29
Alpha Bus. Pk. SO14: South........ 4D 30
Alpha Ho. SO16: Chil 6G 13
Alpine Cl. SO18: South 3B 32
Alpine Cres. PO14: Titch C 6H 49
Alpine Snowsports
Southampton 4A 22
Alton Cl. SO50: Fair O................... 5G 17
Alum Cl. SO45: Holb 5C 54
Alum Way SO18: South 4B 32
Alyne Ho. SO15: South 3B 30
Ambassador Wlk.
SO50: E'leigh.............................. 1H 23
Amberley Cl. SO30: Botl 4E 35
Amberley Cl. SO52: N Bad............2C 12
Amberley Ct. SO40: Tott................5E 27
Amberslade Wlk. SO45: Dib P......5C 52
Amberwood Cl. SO40: Calm.........1B 26
Ambledale SO31: Sar G.................3C 48
Ambleside SO30: Botl....................6B 34
Ambleside Gdns. SO19: South 2A 42
Ambrose Way SO51: Rom 2E 7
American Wharf
SO14: South..................... 4H 5 (1E 41)
Amey Gdns. SO40: Calm 2A 26
Amoy St. SO15: South 5B 30
Ampthill Rd. SO15: South..............4F 29
Ancasta Rd. SO14: South 4D 30
Anchor Bus. Cen. SO53: Cha F.... 2D 14
Andalusian Gdns. PO15: White 5F 45
Anderby Rd. SO16: South 1B 28
Andersen Cl. PO15: White 5G 45
Anderson Cl. SO51: Rom................2F 7
Anderson's Rd.
SO14: South......................5H 5 (2D 40)
Andes Cl. SO14: South 6H 5 (2E 41)
Andes Rd. SO16: Nur 6H 19
Andover Rd. SO15: South............. 5H 29
Andrew Cl. SO40: Tott...................4C 26
Andrew Cl. SO45: Dib P.................5E 53
Andromeda Rd. SO16: South 5C 20
Anfield Cl. SO50: Fair O.................2F 17
Angel Cres. SO18: South 4A 32
Angelica Way PO15: White........... 5H 45
Anglers Way SO31: Lwr Swan......5B 44
Anglesea Ct. SO15: South 2F 29
Anglesea Rd. SO15: South 2F 29
Anglesea Ter.
SO14: South......................5H 5 (2D 40)
Annealing Cl. SO50: E'leigh......... 4H 15
Anson Dr. SO19: South 1C 42
Anson Ho. SO14: South 6G 5 (2D 40)
.............................(off Canute Rd.)
Anson Pl. SO19: South 3E 41
Anstey Rd. SO51: Rom 3E 7
Anton Cl. SO51: Rom.......................5F 7
Anvil Cl. SO30: W End 1C 32
Apollo Pl. SO18: South 3A 32
Apple Ind. Est. PO15: Seg 2G 49
APPLEMORE...................................3A 52
Applemore Health
& Leisure Cen. 3A 52
Appleton Rd. SO18: South........... 2G 31
Appletree Cl. SO40: Calm.............2B 26
Appletree Ct. SO30: Botl 4E 35
Applewood SO31: P Ga 2E 49
Applewood Gdns. SO19: South 2A 42
Applewood Pl. SO40: Tott 5B 26
April Cl. SO18: South....................4B 32
April Gdns. SO45: Blac 5E 55
April Gro. SO31: Sar G..................4C 48
Aquila Way SO31: Hamb 5F 47
Aquitania Ho. SO14: South............6E 31
Arabian Gdns. PO15: White.......... 6G 45
Arakan Cres. SO40: March........... 4D 38
Arbour Ct. PO15: White 4H 45
Arcadia Cl. SO16: South 6G 21
Arcadia Pl. SO17: South 2F 31
Archers SO15: South.....................5A 30
Archers Cl. SO40: Calm.................2C 26
Archers Rd. SO15: South...............4A 30
Archers Rd. SO50: E'leigh 3A 16
Archery Gdns. SO19: South.......... 3H 41
Archery Gro. SO19: South 4G 41
Archery Rd. SO19: South.............. 4G 41
Arden Cl. SO18: South..................2B 32
Ardingly Cres. SO30: Hed E..........2B 34
Ardnave Cres. SO16: Bass 4B 22
Argosy Cl. SO31: Wars 6D 48
Argosy Cres. SO50: E'leigh.......... 1H 23
Argyle Rd. SO14: South..... 1F 5 (6C 30)
Arliss Rd. SO16: South 2E 29
Arlott Ct. SO15: South 3A 30
Arlowe Dr. SO16: South............... 1H 29
Armada Cl. SO16: Rown 2C 20
Armada Dr. SO45: Hythe..............4C 52
Armadale Ho. SO14: South...........5E 31
....(off Kent St.)
Armfield Ho. SO17: South.............2C 30
....(off Winn Rd.)
Armoury, The SO40: March 2E 39
Armstrong Ct. SO16: South......... 4D 20
Arnheim Cl. SO16: South............. 5G 21
Arnheim Rd. SO16: South............. 5H 21
Arnold Rd. SO17: South.................1E 31
Arnold Rd. SO50: E'leigh 1A 24
Arreton SO31: Net A 1C 46
Arrow Cl. SO19: South...................4F 41
Arrow Cl. SO50: E'leigh 2A 16
Arters Lawn SO40: March 5G 37
Arthur Rd. SO15: South 4H 29
Arthur Rd. SO50: E'leigh...............3A 16
Arthurs Gdns. SO30: Hed E 6H 25
Arts Cen. Southampton 2D 4 (6B 30)
Arundel Ho. SO14: South... 1H 5 (5E 31)
Arundel Ho. SO15: South..............3B 30
Arundel Rd. SO40: Tott................. 3G 27
Arundel Rd. SO50: E'leigh 1A 16
Arun Rd. SO18: W End..................6B 24
Ascot Cl. PO14: Titch C 5G 49
Ascot Pl. SO30: Hed E 4H 33
Ascupart Ho. SO17: South........... 3D 30
Ascupart St.
SO14: South......................3G 5 (1D 40)
.... (not continuous)
Asford Gro. SO50: B'stke..............3C 16
Ashbridge Ri. SO53: Cha F.............4C 8
Ashburnham Cl. SO19: South.......6F 31
Ashburton Cl. SO45: Dib 3B 52
Ashby Cres. SO40: Tott 4C 26
Ashby Rd. SO19: South 2B 42
Ashby Rd. SO40: Tott 4C 26
Ash Cl. SO19: South 5C 32
Ash Cl. SO21: Col C 5F 11
Ash Cl. SO31: Burs 5F 43
Ash Cl. SO51: Rom 6F 7
Ashcombe Ho. SO14: South 5E 31
.............................(off Meridian Way)
Ash Ct. SO19: South 2H 41
Ashcroft Ct. SO53: Cha F 1F 15
Ashdene SO15: South....................3F 29
Ashdene Rd. SO40: A'hst 3B 36
Ashdown SO45: F'ley 3F 55
Ashdown Cl. SO53: Cha F 3E 9
Ashdown Dr. SO53: Cha F 3E 9
Ashdown Rd. SO45: F'ley...............3F 55
Ashdown Rd. SO53: Cha F 3E 9
Ashdown Way SO51: Rom 5E 7
Ashen Cl. SO53: Cha F 5E 9
Ashfield Vw. SO52: N Bad 2E 13
Ashford Cres. SO45: Hythe............3F 53
Ash Gro. SO40: A'hst.....................2B 36
Ashlea Cl. SO50: Fair O 2G 17
Ashleigh Cl. SO45: Hythe 6E 53
Ashlett Cl. SO45: F'ley.................. 2H 55
Ashlett M. SO45: F'ley.................. 2H 55
Ashlett Rd. SO45: F'ley................. 2H 55
Ashley Cl. SO31: Swanw 6F 45
Ashley Ct. SO31: Burs 3G 43
Ashley Cres. SO19: South 3C 42
Ashley Cross Cl. SO45: Holb 5C 54
Ashley Gdns. SO53: Cha F............ 2G 15
Ashley Ho. SO51: Rom 5B 6
Ashmead Rd. SO16: South 6D 20
Ashridge Cl. SO15: South..............3B 30
Ash Rd. SO40: A'hst 3A 36
Ashton Gdns. SO50: E'leigh...........3B 16
Ashtree Ct. SO53: Cha F................4E 15
Ash Tree Rd. SO18: South 2G 31
ASHURST 3B 36
ASHURST BRIDGE 6B 26
Ashurst Bri. Rd. SO40: Tott 5B 26
Ashurst Campsite SO40: A'hst.....5A 36
ASHURST CHILD
& FAMILY CEN. 4A 36
Ashurst Cl. SO19: South 4A 42
Ashurst Cl. SO40: A'hst 3B 36
Ashurst New Forest
Station (Rail)..................................4A 36
Ash Way PO15: White................... 5H 45
Ashwood PO15: White 2H 49
Ashwood SO31: Loc H.................. 5G 49
Ashwood Gdns. SO16: South 6A 22
Ashwood Gdns. SO40: Tott 5C 26
Aspen Av. SO31: Wars...................1B 50
Aspen Cl. SO21: Col C 5G 11
Aspen Cl. SO30: Hed E 5B 34
Aspen Holt SO16: Bass..................4C 22
Aspen Wlk. SO40: Tott 3B 26
Aster Rd. SO16: S'ing 5E 23
Astra Ct. SO45: Hythe....................1E 53
Astral Gdns. SO31: Hamb..............4F 47
Asturias Way
SO14: South..................... 6H 5 (2E 41)
Asylum Rd. SO15: South 5C 30
Atheling Rd. SO45: Hythe..............3E 53
Athelstan Rd. SO19: South.......... 4G 31
Athena Cl. SO50: Fair O 5G 17
Atherfield Rd. SO16: South 6C 20
Atherley Bowling Club..................3A 30
Atherley Ct. SO15: South..............3A 30
Atherley Rd. SO15: South............. 5H 29
Atlantic Cl. SO14: South.............. 3D 40
Atlantic Pk. Vw. SO18: W End......6A 24
Atlantic Way SO14: South 3C 40
Auckland Rd. SO15: South........... 4D 28
Audley Pl. SO50: B'stke.................6E 17
Augustine Rd.
SO14: South......................1H 5 (5D 30)
Augustus Cl. SO53: Cha F 6G 9
Augustus Way SO53: Cha F 6G 9
Austen Gdns. PO15: White 5G 45
Austen Hgts. SO19: South............3F 41
.... (off Capstan Rd.)
Authie Grn. SO52: N Bad...............3E 13
Autumn Pl. SO17: South................2C 30
Autumn Rd. SO40: March..............4E 39
Avebury Gdns. SO53: Cha F 4C 8
Avenger Cl. SO53: Cha F 2D 14
Avenue, The SO14: South...............4C 30
Avenue, The SO17: South..............6B 22
Avenue C SO45: Hard 6H 53
Avenue Ct. SO17: South 3B 30
Avenue D SO45: Hard 6H 53
Avenue E SO45: Hard 6H 53
Avenue Rd. SO14: South 3C 30
Avery Flds. SO50: E'leigh 6B 10
Avington Cl. SO50: B'stke 2E 17
Avington Ct. SO16: Bass 5B 22
Avonborne Way SO53: Cha F 5C 8
Avon Ct. SO31: Net A.....................2B 46
Avon Cres. SO51: Rom 5F 7
Avondale Ct. SO17: South 1D 30
Avondale Mobile Home Pk.
SO21: Col C................................ 5G 11
Avon Grn. SO53: Cha F..................2F 15
Avon Ho. SO14: South 5E 31
Avon Rd. SO18: South 2H 31
Avon Way SO30: W End.................1E 33
Avro Cl. SO15: South 4E 29
Avro Ct. SO31: Hamb.....................5F 47
Ayerswood SO30: Hed E.............. 1H 43
Aynsley Ct. SO15: South.............. 4H 29

B

Back of the Walls
SO14: South...................... 6E 5 (2C 40)
.... (not continuous)
Bacon Cl. SO19: South 4H 41
Baddesley Pk. Ind. Est.
SO52: N Bad 3F 13
Baddesley Rd. SO52: N Bad...........5C 8
Baddesley Rd. SO53: Cha F 4C 8
Baden Powell Ho. SO51: Rom 5B 6
.... (off Baden Powell Way)
Baden Powell Way SO51: Rom 5B 6
Bader Cl. SO30: Hed E...................3A 34
Badger Cl. SO50: B'stke.................6E 17
Badger Ct. SO50: B'stke.................6E 17
Badgers, The SO31: Net A.............1C 46
Badgers Copse SO31: P Ga............2F 49
Badgers Run SO31: Sar G 1C 48

A-Z Southampton 57

Blackfield Rd. – Budds Cl.

Blackfield Rd. SO45: Blac 4E 55
Blackfield Rd. SO45: F'ley 4E 55
Blackthorn Cl. SO19: South 6H 31
Blackthorn Grn. SO21: Col C 5G 11
Blackthorn Rd. SO19: South 6G 31
Blackwater Dr. SO40: Tott 2C 26
Blackwater M. SO40: Tott 2C 26
Bladon Rd. SO16: South 1G 29
Blake Bldg., The
SO14: South 6H 5 (3D 40)
Blake Cl. PO15: White 4F 45
Blake Cl. SO16: Nur 4B 20
Blake Gdns. SO19: South 2B 42
Blakeney Rd. SO16: South 1B 28
Blandford Ho. SO16: South 2D 28
Blann Cl. SO16: Nur 4A 20
Bleaklow Cl. SO16: South 3D 28
BLECHYNDEN 2B 4 (6A 30)
Blechynden Ter.
SO15: South 2B 4 (6A 30)
Blencowe Dr. SO53: Cha F 2A 14
Blendworth La. SO18: South 4C 32
Blenheim Av. SO17: South 2C 30
Blenheim Cl. SO53: Cha F 3B 14
Blenheim Ct. SO17: South 2C 30
Blenheim Gdns. SO17: South 1D 30
Blenheim Gdns. SO45: Dib P 5B 52
Blenheim Ho. SO50: E'leigh 5B 16
Blenheim Ho. SO51: Rom 5E 7
(off Chambers Av.)
Blenheim Rd. SO50: E'leigh 5A 16
Blighmont Av. SO15: South 5F 29
Blighmont Cres. SO15: South 5F 29
Blind La. SO30: W End 4H 25
Blind La. SO32: Curd 1H 35
Bloomsbury Wlk. SO19: South 3G 41
Blossom Cl. SO30: Botl 5C 34
Blue Anchor La.
SO14: South 5D 4 (2B 40)
Bluebell Cl. SO31: Loc H 5D 48
Bluebell Ct. PO15: White 5H 45
Bluebell Gdns. SO45: Hythe 4F 53
Bluebell Rd. SO16: Bass 5D 22
Bluebell Rd. SO16: S'ing 5D 22
Bluebell Way PO15: White 4H 45
Bluestar Gdns. SO30: Hed E 1A 34
Blundell La. SO31: Burs 3H 43
Blyth Cl. SO16: South 1B 28
Blythe Gdns. SO30: Hed E 1G 43
Boakes Pl. SO40: A'hst 3B 36
Boardwalk Way SO40: March 2E 39
Bodding Av. SO16: Nur 5B 20
Bodmin Rd. SO50: B'stke 4E 17
Bodycoats Rd. SO53: Cha F 1F 15
Bolderwood Cl. SO50: B'stke 5E 17
Boldrewood Rd. SO16: Bass 5A 22
Bolhinton Av. SO40: March 4B 38
Bonchurch Cl. SO16: S'ing 4E 23
Bond Rd. SO18: South 2G 31
Bond St. SO14: South 5E 31
Boniface Cl. SO40: Tott 3C 26
Boniface Cres. SO16: South 6B 20
BOORLEY GREEN 2D 34
Boorley Grn. Development
SO32: Botl 1E 35
Boothby Cl. SO40: Elin 5G 27
Borden Way SO52: N Bad 3E 13
Borrowdale Rd. SO16: South 2C 28
Bossington Cl. SO16: Rown 4C 20
Boston Cl. PO14: Titch 5H 49
Boston Ct. SO53: Cha F 6F 9
Bosville SO50: E'leigh 1H 15
Boswell Cl. SO19: South 5C 32
Boswell Cl. SO30: Botl 5E 35
BOTANY BAY 3A 42
Botany Bay Rd. SO19: South 2B 42
BOTLEY 5E 35
Botley Gdns. SO19: South 2E 43
Botley Hill SO30: Botl 5F 35
Botley Mills Craft & Bus. Cen.
SO30: Botl 5E 35
Botley Rd. SO16: Chil 4G 13
Botley Rd. SO19: South 3C 42
Botley Rd. SO30: Hed E 2E 33
Botley Rd. SO30: W End 2E 33
Botley Rd. SO31: Burr 5E 45
Botley Rd. SO31: Swanw 5E 45
Botley Rd. SO32: Bis W 4G 35
Botley Rd. SO32: Curd 4G 35
Botley Rd. SO50: Fair O 2G 17
Botley Rd. SO50: Hor H 2G 17
Botley Rd. SO51: Rom 5C 6
Botley Rd. SO52: N Bad 2E 13
Botley Station (Rail) 4G 35
Bottings Ind. Est. SO30: Curd 4G 35
Boundary Acre SO31: Burs 1H 43
Boundary Cl. SO15: South 4D 28
Boundary Lakes Golf Course 3F 33
Boundary Rd. SO31: Burs 5F 43
(not continuous)
Boundstone SO45: Hythe 4C 52
Bourne Av. SO15: South 2G 29
Bourne Cl. SO21: Ott 2C 10
Bournemouth Rd. SO53: Cha F 5D 14
Bourne Rd. SO15: South 1A 4 (6H 29)
Bowater Cl. SO40: Calm 2C 26
Bowater Way SO40: Calm 2C 26
Bowcombe SO31: Net A 6C 42
Bowden Ho. SO17: South 1E 31
Bowden La. SO17: South 1E 31
Bower Cl. SO19: South 4H 41
Bower Cl. SO45: Holb 5B 54
Bowers Dr. SO31: Burs 3F 43
Bow Lake Gdns. SO50: B'stke 2D 16
Bow Lake Wlk. SO50: B'stke 2D 16
Bowland Ri. SO53: Cha F 6B 8
Bowland Way SO45: Blac 5E 55
Bowman Ct. SO19: South
Florence Rd. 2F 41
Bowman Ct. SO19: South
Range Gdns. 2B 42
Boyatt Cres. SO50: E'leigh 5A 10
Boyatt La. SO21: Ott 4A 10
Boyatt La. SO50: E'leigh 5A 10
BOYATT WOOD 2A 16
Boyes La. SO21: Col C 4G 11
(not continuous)
Boyton Mead SO50: E'leigh 6C 10
Brabant Cl. PO15: White 6F 45
Brabazon Rd. PO15: Seg 2H 49
Bracken Cl. SO52: N Bad 4E 13
Bracken Cres. SO50: B'stke 6E 17
Bracken Hall SO16: Chil 1D 22
Bracken La. SO16: South 2E 29
Bracken Pl. SO16: Chil 2C 22
Bracken Rd. SO52: N Bad 4E 13
Brackens, The SO31: Loc H 5F 49
Brackens, The SO45: Dib P 4B 52
Brackenway Rd. SO53: Cha F 5E 9
Bracklesham Cl. SO19: South 2H 41
Brackley Av. SO50: Fair O 5G 17
Brading Cl. SO16: S'ing 4E 23
Bradley Grn. SO16: South 5F 21
Bradshaw Cl. SO50: Fair O 1H 17
Braehead SO45: Hythe 4C 52
Braeside Cl. SO19: South 6G 31
Braeside Cres. SO19: South 6G 31
Braeside Rd. SO19: South 6G 31
Braishfield Cl. SO16: South 2D 28
Bramble Cl. SO45: Holb 5C 54
Bramble Cl. SO50: E'leigh 2B 16
Bramble Dr. SO51: Rom 4F 7
Bramble Hill SO53: Cha F 1D 14
Bramble La. SO31: Sar G 2C 48
Bramble M. SO18: South 3A 32
Brambles, The SO40: Tott 1E 27
Brambles Cl. SO21: Col C 5G 11
Brambling Cl. SO16: South 3F 21
Bramblings, The SO40: Tott 4B 26
BRAMBRIDGE 5F 11
Brambridge SO50: B'dge 5E 11
Brambridge Pk. 4E 11
Bramdean M. SO19: South 6G 31
Bramdean Rd. SO18: South 3D 32
Bramley Cres. SO19: South 3B 42
Bramley Ho. SO30: Hed E 5H 33
Brampton Mnr. SO16: Bass 4B 22
Brampton Twr. SO16: Bass 4B 22
Bramshott Rd. SO19: South 5H 41
Bramston Rd. SO15: South 3G 29
Bramtoco Way SO40: Tott 4E 27
Bramwell Ct. SO19: South 5B 32
Branewick Cl. PO15: Seg 4H 49
Branksome Av. SO15: South 2G 29
Bransbury Cl. SO16: South 5G 21
Bransley Cl. SO51: Rom 3E 7
Brasenose Cl. PO14: Titch C 6G 49
Brasher Cl. SO50: B'stke 5F 17
Breach La. SO50: B'stke 2D 16
Breamore Cl. SO50: E'leigh 1A 16
Breamore Rd. SO18: South 4D 32
Brean Cl. SO16: South 1C 28
Brecon Cl. SO45: Dib P 4B 52
Brecon Cl. SO53: Cha F 4D 14
Brecon Ho. SO19: South 3F 41
Brecon Rd. SO19: South 6C 32
Brendon Cl. SO45: Dib P 4A 52
Brendon Grn. SO16: South 3D 28
Brentwood Cres. SO18: South 2A 32
Breton Cl. PO15: White 6F 45
Brewer Cl. SO31: Loc H 3F 49
Brewery La. SO51: Rom 5B 6
Briardene Ct. SO40: Tott 4E 27
Briarswood SO16: South 2F 29
Briarswood Ri. SO45: Dib P 4A 52
Briar Way SO51: Rom 4F 7
Briarwood Rd. SO40: Tott 5B 26
Brickfield La. SO53: Cha F 2D 14
Brickfield Rd. SO17: South 1E 31
Brickfield Trad. Est.
SO53: Cha F 2E 15
Brick La. SO51: Rom 5C 6
Brickmakers Rd. SO21: Col C 5F 11
Brickwoods Cl. SO51: Rom 4E 7
Bridge Cl. SO31: Burs 4H 43
Bridge Ct. SO51: Rom 5A 6
Bridge Rd. SO19: South 2F 41
Bridge Rd. SO31: Burs 4H 43
Bridge Rd. SO31: Lwr Swan 1C 48
Bridge Rd. SO31: P Ga 1C 48
Bridge Rd. SO31: Sar G 1C 48
Bridge Rd. SO51: Rom 5C 6
Bridgers Cl. SO16: Rown 4C 20
Bridges Cl. SO50: E'leigh 4H 15
Bridge Ter.
SO14: South 6H 5 (2D 40)
Bridgwater Ct. SO15: South 5G 29
Bridlington Av. SO15: South 3H 29
Bridport Ct. SO15: South 6G 29
Brigantine Rd. SO31: Wars 6C 48
Brighstone Cl. SO16: S'ing 4E 23
Brighton Rd. SO15: South 4B 30
Brightside Rd. SO16: South 1D 28
Bright Wire Cres.
SO50: E'leigh 5H 15
Brindle Cl. SO16: Bass 4C 22
Brinsley Cl. SO19: South 6C 32
Brinton La. SO45: Hythe 2E 53
Brinton's Rd.
SO14: South 1F 5 (6C 30)
Brinton's Ter. SO14: South 5C 30
Britannia Ct.
SO14: South 2H 5 (6E 31)
Britannia Gdns. SO30: Hed E 6H 25
Britannia Rd.
SO14: South 1H 5 (6D 30)
Britannia Wharf
SO14: South 3H 5 (1E 41)
Britannic Ho. SO14: South 6E 31
(off Kent St.)
Briton St. SO14: South 6E 5 (2C 40)
Brittany Cl. SO40: March 4D 38
Broadbent Cl. SO16: Rown 3B 20
Broad Grn. SO14: South 3F 5 (1C 40)
Broadlands Av. SO50: E'leigh 1A 16
Broadlands Lake 5E 19
Broadlands Rd. SO17: South 5D 22
Broad La. SO52: N Bad 2C 12
Broadleaf Cl. SO45: Dib P 5B 52
Broadley Cl. SO45: Holb 4B 54
Broadmeadow Cl. SO40: Tott 4E 27
Broadmead Rd. SO16: Nur 3B 20
Broad Oak SO30: Botl 4C 34
BROADOAK 4D 34
Broadoak Cl. SO45: Holb 5B 54
Broadwater Rd. SO18: South 6H 23
Broadwater Rd. SO51: Rom 5A 6
Broadway SO31: Hamb 2E 47
Broadway, The SO17: South 2D 30
Broadway, The SO18: South 4D 32
Brocks Cl. SO45: Dib P 5A 52
Brokenford Av. SO40: Tott 4G 27
Brokenford Bus. Cen.
SO40: Tott 4F 27
Brokenford La. SO40: Tott 4F 27
Bromley Rd. SO18: South 2H 31
Bronte Cl. SO40: Tott 5C 26
Bronte Gdns. PO15: White 5G 45
Bronte Way SO19: South 5G 31
Brook Av. SO31: Wars 4A 48
Brook Cl. SO31: Sar G 4B 48
Brook Cl. SO52: N Bad 4E 13
Brook Cl. SO53: Cha F 3E 15
Brook Ct. SO15: South 6H 29
BROOKE'S HILL 5A 18
Brookes Hill Ind. Est.
SO40: Calm 6A 18
Brookfield Gdns. SO31: Sar G 3D 48
Brookfield Pl. SO17: South 1D 30
Brook Ho. SO19: South 2A 42
Brook La. SO30: Botl 5D 34
Brook La. SO31: Sar G 3E 49
Brook La. SO31: Sar G 6A 48
Brook La. SO31: Wars 6A 48
Brooklyn Cl. SO21: Ott 2C 10
Brooklyn Ct. SO21: Ott 2C 10
(off Main Rd.)
Brook Rd. SO18: South 4A 32
Brook Rd. SO50: Fair O 1F 17
Brookside SO40: Tott 6F 27
Brookside Av. SO15: South 4D 28
Brookside Dr. SO31: Sar G 4B 48
Brookside Ho. SO18: S'ing 5G 23
Brookside Way SO18: S'ing 5G 23
Brookside Way SO30: W End 1E 33
Brookvale Ct. SO17: South 2C 30
Brookvale Rd. SO17: South 2C 30
Brook Valley SO16: South 1E 29
Brook Wlk. SO40: Calm 2B 26
Brookwood Av. SO50: E'leigh 4H 15
Brookwood Ind. Est.
SO50: E'leigh 4A 16
Brookwood Rd. SO16: South 3B 28
Brooms Gro. SO19: South 2D 42
Broomy Cl. SO45: Dib 3A 52
Broughton Cl. SO16: South 2E 29
Broughton Ho. SO18: South 3G 31
Brownhill Cl. SO53: Cha F 6E 9
Brownhill Ct. SO16: South 6C 20
Brownhill Gdns. SO53: Cha F 6E 9
Brownhill Ho. SO16: South 6C 20
Brownhill Rd. SO52: N Bad 3E 13
(not continuous)
Brownhill Rd. SO53: Cha F 6E 9
Brownhill Way SO16: Nur 6A 20
Browning Av. SO19: South 5D 32
Browning Cl. PO15: White 4G 45
Browning Cl. SO40: Tott 4C 26
Browning Cl. SO50: E'leigh 4H 15
Brownlow Av. SO19: South 5H 31
Brownlow Gdns. SO19: South 5A 32
Brownwich La. PO14: Titch 5G 51
Browsholme Cl. SO50: E'leigh 1A 16
Broxburn Cl. SO53: Cha F 5G 9
Brunei Ho. SO16: Bass 4C 22
Brunel Cl. SO30: Hed E 2B 34
Brunel Rd. SO15: South 3A 28
Brunel Way PO15: Seg 2H 49
Brunswick Cl. SO50: Fair O 5G 17
Brunswick Pl.
SO15: South 1D 4 (5B 30)
Brunswick Pl. SO40: Tott 4E 27
Brunswick Rd. SO50: Fair O 5G 17
Brunswick Sq.
SO14: South 6E 5 (2C 40)
Bryanston Rd. SO19: South 6F 31
Bryony Cl. SO31: Loc H 5D 48
Bubb La. SO30: W End 6H 25
Buchanan Rd. SO16: South 4D 20
Buchan Av. PO15: White 5G 45
Buchan Ct. SO45: Dib P 4A 52
Buckingham Ct. SO17: South 3C 30
(off Westwood Rd.)
Buckland Cl. SO50: E'leigh 1A 16
Buckland Gdns. SO40: Calm 1B 26
Buckley Ct. SO16: South 2F 29
Buckthorn Cl. SO40: Tott 3A 26
Budds Cl. SO30: Hed E 2A 34

A-Z Southampton 59

Budds La. – Chantry Wlk.

Budds La. SO51: Rom 4A **6**
Budds La. Ind. Est. SO51: Rom 3A **6**
Bugle St. SO14: South 6D **4** (2B **40**)
Bullar Rd. SO18: South................ 4G **31**
Bullar St. SO14: South................ 5D **30**
Bullfinch Cl. SO40: Tott................4B **26**
Bullrush Cl. SO45: Dib P...............5C **52**
Bulls Copse Rd. SO40: Tott..........1F **37**
Burbush Cl. SO45: Holb.................5C **54**
Burgess Ct. SO16: Bass 5D **22**
Burgess Gdns. SO16: South.........6A **22**
Burgess Rd. SO16: Bass .... 6H **21** .... (not continuous)
Burgess Rd. SO16: South............ 6H **21** .... (not continuous)
Burgess Rd. SO17: Bass 5C **22**
Burgess Rd. SO17: S'ing 5C **22**
Burghclere Rd. SO19: South 5H **41**
Burgoyne Rd. SO19: South...........1E **43**
Burgundy Cl. SO31: Loc H........... 5D **48**
Burke Dr. SO19: South..................5C **32**
Burley Cl. SO40: Tott....................4A **26**
Burley Cl. SO53: Cha F................ 3D **14**
Burley Ct. SO17: South................1C **30**
Burley Down SO53: Cha F............ 3D **14**
Burlington Ct. SO19: South 6B **32**
Burlington Ho. SO30: Hed E 3B **34**
Burlington Mans. SO15: South.... 4G **29**
Burlington Rd. SO15: South 5A **30**
Burma Ho. SO18: S'ing................ 5G **23**
Burma Rd. SO51: Rom 5B **6**
Burma Way SO40: March 4D **38**
Burmese Cl. PO15: White 6G **45**
Burnbank Gdns. SO40: Tott 4E **27**
Burnett Cl. SO18: South 2G **31**
Burnett Cl. SO45: Hythe................4F **53**
Burnetts La. SO30: W End........... 6G **25**
Burney Pl. SO31: Sar G 3D **48**
Burnham Beeches SO53: Cha F.......................... 1D **14**
Burnham Chase SO18: South.......4B **32**
Burns Cl. SO50: E'leigh................ 6G **15**
Burns Pl. SO16: South...................1E **29**
Burns Rd. SO19: South.................. 5D **32**
Burns Rd. SO50: E'leigh 6H **15**
Burr Cl. SO21: Col C 5F **11**
BURRIDGE....................................4F **45**
Burridge Rd. SO30: Botl 5G **35**
Burridge Rd. SO30: Curd............... 5G **35**
Burridge Rd. SO31: Burr.................3E **45**
Burrow Hill Pl. SO50: B'stke 2D **16**
BURSLEDON 5H **43**
Bursledon Brickworks Industrial Mus. **5C 44**
BURSLEDON HALL..........................**3A 44**
Bursledon Hgts. SO31: Burs........ 4H **43**
Bursledon Rd. SO19: South..........5A **32**
Bursledon Rd. SO30: Hed E.......... 1H **43**
Bursledon Rd. SO31: Burs.............. 3G **43**
Bursledon Station (Rail) 5A **44**
Bursledon Windmill........................**3G 43**
Burton Rd. SO15: South 5A **30**
Bury Brickfield Pk. Cvn. Site SO40: Elin 1A **38**
Bury La. SO40: Elin........................ 6H **27**
Bury Rd. SO40: March....................2B **38**
Busketts Way SO40: A'hst 3A **36**
BUTLOCKS HEATH 1C **46**
Buttercup Cl. SO30: Hed E 5G **33**
Buttercup Cl. SO45: Hythe 5E **53**
Buttercup Way SO31: Loc H..........4C **48**
Butterfield Rd. SO16: Bass...........6A **22**
Buttermere Cl. SO16: South 1C **28**
BUTTSASH......................................6E **53**
Butts Ash Av. SO45: Hythe 6E **53**
Butts Ash Gdns. SO45: Hythe.......6E **53**
Butts Bri. Hill SO45: Hythe 4E **53**
Buttsbridge Rd. SO45: Hythe 5E **53**
Butt's Cl. SO19: South 1D **42**
Butt's Cres. SO19: South...............1C **42**
Butt's Rd. SO19: South..................3B **42**
Butt's Sq. SO19: South 1C **42**
Byam's La. SO40: March 3E **39**
Bye Rd. SO31: Lwr Swan................5B **44**
Byeways SO45: Hythe 4C **52**
Byron Ct. SO15: South...................5A **30**
Byron Rd. SO19: South...................5C **32**
Byron Rd. SO50: E'leigh 3B **16**
By The Wood SO40: Calm 1C **26**

C

Cable St. SO14: South 1H **5** (6E **31**)
Cable St. SO50: E'leigh.................5A **16**
Cabot Cl. SO31: Loc H 4C **48**
Cabot Dr. SO45: Dib.......................3A **52**
Cabot Ho. SO14: South ......4G **5** (1D **40**) ....*(off The Compass)*
Cadland Ct. SO14: South ... 6H **5** (2E **41**)
Cadland Pk. Est. SO45: Hard........3C **54**
Cadland Rd. SO45: Hard................2B **54**
Caerleon Av. SO19: South 5C **32**
Caerleon Dr. SO19: South..............5B **32**
Caernarvon Gdns. SO53: Cha F.....3C **14**
Caigers Grn. SO31: Burr 4F **45**
Caistor Cl. SO16: South 5E **21**
Calabrese SO31: Swanw 6F **45**
Calbourne SO31: Net A..................6C **42**
Calder Cl. SO16: South 3C **28**
Calderwood Dr. SO19: South.........1A **42**
Caledonia Dr. SO45: Dib 3B **52**
California Cl. SO40: Tott................2A **26**
CALMORE 1B **26**
Calmore Cres. SO40: Calm............1A **26**
Calmore Cres. SO40: Tott..............1A **26**
Calmore Dr. SO40: Calm.................2B **26**
Calmore Gdns. SO40: Tott.............4C **26**
Calmore Ind. Est. SO40: Tott.........1E **27** .... (not continuous)
Calmore Rd. SO40: Calm................1B **26**
Calshot Ct. SO14: South 3E **41**
Calshot Dr. SO53: Cha F 4C **14**
Calshot Rd. SO45: F'ley.................. 2H **55**
Camargue Cl. PO15: White 5F **45**
Camborne Cl. SO50: B'stke 5E **17**
Cambria Dr. SO45: Dib 3A **52**
Cambrian Cl. SO31: Burs............... 3G **43**
Cambridge Dr. SO53: Cha F ....4E **15** .... (not continuous)
Cambridge Grn. PO14: Titch C 5G **49**
Cambridge Grn. SO53: Cha F 4E **15**
Cambridge Rd. SO14: South..........3C **30**
Camelia Gdns. SO18: South 1A **32**
Camelia Gro. SO50: Fair O............ 1H **17**
Camellia Cl. SO52: N Bad 3E **13**
Camellia Ho. SO14: South .6G **5** (2D **40**) .... *(off Royal Cres. Rd.)*
Camellia Way PO15: White............ 5H **45**
Cameron Ct. SO16: South.............. 4D **20**
Camilla Cl. SO40: Calm 2A **26**
Camino Ct. PO14: Titch C 6H **49**
Camley Cl. SO19: South................. 4G **41**
Campbell Rd. SO50: E'leigh...........6B **16**
Campbell Way SO50: Fair O 1F **17**
Campion Cl. SO31: Wars 6C **48**
Campion Dr. SO51: Rom.................3F **7**
Campion Rd. SO19: South 6D **32**
Canada Pl. SO16: Bass...................5A **22**
Canada Rd. SO19: South 3G **41**
Canal Cl. SO51: Rom 4C **6**
Canal Wlk. SO14: South 5E **5** (2C **40**)
Canal Wlk. SO51: Rom 5B **6**
Canberra Rd. SO16: Nur.............. 5H **19**
Canberra Towers SO19: South 5H **41**
Candlemas Pl. SO17: South 3C **30**
Candover Ct. SO19: South.............5A **42**
Candy La. SO18: South...................4E **33**
Canford Cl. SO16: South.................1B **28**
Cannon St. SO15: South 3G **29**
Canoe Cl. SO31: Wars.................... 6D **48**
Canon Ct. SO50: Fair O.................. 2G **17**
Canon Pl. SO19: South 6D **32**
Cantell Community Sports Cen. **5C 22**
Canterbury Av. SO19: South..........2C **42**
Canterbury Dr. SO45: Dib 3A **52**
Canton St. SO15: South.................5B **30**
Canute Ho. SO14: South .... 5F **5** (2C **40**) ....*(off King St.)*
Canute Rd. SO14: South.....6G **5** (2D **40**)
Canvey Ct. SO16: South..................1C **28**
Capella Gdns. SO45: Dib 3B **52**
Capon Cl. SO18: S'ing 5G **23**
Capstan Gdns. SO31: Loc H 4G **49**
Capstan Rd. SO19: South 3F **41**
Captain's Pl. SO14: South.......................6G **5** (2D **40**)
Caraway PO15: White................... 6H **45**
Cardinal Pl. SO16: South............... 1D **28**
Cardinal Way SO31: Loc H 4F **49**
Cardington Ct. SO16: South 5D **20**
Carey Rd. SO19: South 6C **32**
Carisbrooke SO31: Net A.............6C **42**
Carisbrooke Cres. SO53: Cha F... 2G **15**
Carisbrooke Dr. SO19: South 5H **31**
Carlisle Rd. SO16: South...............3F **29**
Carlton Commerce Cen., The SO14: South.................................. 4D **30**
Carlton Ct. SO15: South.................3B **30**
Carlton Cres. SO15: South.............5B **30**
Carlton Pl. SO15: South..................5B **30**
Carlton Rd. SO15: South................4B **30**
Carlyn Dr. SO53: Cha F....................6F **9**
Carnation Rd. SO16: S'ing............4E **23**
Carne Cl. SO53: Cha F......................5E **9**
Caroline Ct. SO15: South..............3F **29**
Carolyn Cl. SO19: South 3G **41**
Carpathia Cl. SO18: W End...........1A **32**
Carpathia Ct. SO14: South .... 6E **5** (2C **40**) ....*(off Briton St.)*
Carpathia Dr. SO14: South.....................5G **5** (2D **40**)
Carpenter Cl. SO45: Hythe............3E **53**
Carpenters Cl. SO30: Hed E 1H **43**
Carpenter Wlk. SO45: F'ley 3F **55**
Carpiquet Pk. SO52: N Bad 3E **13**
Carrington Ho. SO17: South 2C **30**
Carrol Cl. SO50: Fair O 2G **17**
Carroll Cl. PO15: White 4G **45**
Carronades, The SO14: South..................... 2F **5** (6C **30**) ....*(off New Rd.)*
Carthage Cl. SO53: Cha F............. 6H **9**
Caspian Cl. PO15: White...............6F **45**
Castilian Way PO15: White............6F **45**
Castle Ct. SO15: South 5E **29**
Castle Ho. SO14: South .....5D **4** (2B **40**) ....*(off Castle Way)*
Castle La. SO14: South......5D **4** (2B **40**) .... (not continuous)
Castle La. SO52: Cha F..................3F **13**
Castle La. SO52: N Bad 3F **13**
Castle La. SO53: Cha F..................3C **14**
Castle Pl. SO14: South.......6D **4** (2B **40**) ....*(off High St.)*
Castle Rd. SO18: South 1G **31**
Castle Rd. SO31: Net A...................1B **46**
Castleshaw Cl. SO16: South........ 4D **28**
Castle Sq. SO14: South 5D **4** (2B **40**)
Castle St. SO14: South 4C **30**
Castle Way SO14: South.... 4D **4** (1B **40**)
Castlewood SO53: Cha F............. 3D **14**
Catamaran Cl. SO31: Wars........... 6D **48**
Cateran Cl. SO16: South............... 3D **28**
Cathay Gdns. SO45: Dib 3A **52**
Catherine Cl. SO30: W End...........1E **33**
Catherine Gdns. SO30: W End......1E **33**
Causeway SO51: Rom 5A **6**
Causeway Cres. SO40: Tott.......... 3G **27**
Causton Gdns. SO50: E'leigh........4A **16**
Cavalier Cl. SO45: Dib 3A **52**
Cavell Pl. SO19: South................... 4H **41**
Cavendish Cl. SO51: Rom 3E **7**
Cavendish Dr. SO31: Loc H 4C **48**
Cavendish Gro. SO17: South 3B **30**
Cavendish M. SO15: South.............3B **30**
C Av. SO45: F'ley 2C **54**
Caversham Cl. SO19: South 1A **42**
Caversham Cl. SO30: W End 3D **32**
Cawte Rd. SO15: South 5G **29**
Cawtes Reach SO31: Wars...........4B **48**
Caxton Av. SO19: South.................5B **32**
Cecil Av. SO16: South....................2F **29**
Cecil Av. SO40: A'hst.....................3B **36**
Cecil Gdns. SO31: Sar G................3E **49**
Cecil Rd. SO19: South 2H **41**
Cedar Av. SO15: South 3G **29**
Cedar Cl. SO30: Hed E...................5A **34**
Cedar Cl. SO31: Burs.....................5F **43**
Cedar Gdns. SO14: South 3C **30**
Cedar Lawn SO51: Rom 3F **7**
Cedar Lodge SO15: South 3E **29**
Cedar Rd. SO14: South..................3C **30**
Cedar Rd. SO45: Hythe 6E **53**
Cedar Rd. SO50: E'leigh 6G **15**
Cedar Wood Cl. SO50: Fair O 1H **17**
Cedarwood Cl. SO40: Calm..........3B **26**
Cedric Cl. SO45: Blac 5F **55**
Celandine Av. SO31: Loc H.......... 5D **48**
Celandine Cl. SO53: Cha F 2B **14**
Cement Ter. SO14: South.......................5D **4** (2B **40**)
Cemetery Rd. SO15: South...........3A **30**
Centenary Plaza SO19: South 3E **41**
Centenary Quay SO19: South.......3E **41**
Central Bri. SO14: South ...5G **5** (2D **40**)
Central Cres. SO40: March...........2E **39**
Central Rd. SO14: South.... 6F **5** (3C **40**)
Central Sta. Bri. ....**2A 4 (6A 30)**
Central Trad. Est. SO14: South.....................3H **5** (1D **40**)
Centre 27 Retail Pk......................**2G** 33
Centre Ct. SO15: South..................3F **29**
Centre Way SO31: Loc H 4D **48**
Centurion Ind. Pk. SO18: South ... 4E **31**
Century Ct. SO14: South.... 6E **5** (2C **40**) ....*(off Lwr. Canal Wlk.)*
Cerdic M. SO31: Hamb 3G **47**
Cerne Cl. SO18: W End 2B **32**
Cerne Cl. SO52: N Bad...................3C **12**
Chadwell Av. SO19: South.............1B **42**
Chadwick Rd. SO50: E'leigh........ 5H **15**
Chadwick Way SO31: Hamb 5F **47**
Chafen Rd. SO18: South 3F **31**
Chaffinch Cl. SO40: Tott...............3B **26**
Chalcroft Distribution Pk. SO30: W End................................. 4H **25**
Chalewood Rd. SO45: Blac 5E **55**
Chalfont Ct. SO16: South...............2E **29**
Chalice Ct. SO30: Hed E 5H **33**
Chalk Hill SO18: W End 3C **32**
Challenger Pl. SO45: Dib P...........4A **52**
Challenger Way SO45: Dib............2A **52**
Challenger Way SO45: Dib P..........2A **52**
Challis Ct. SO14: South 5F **5** (2C **40**)
Chalmers Way SO31: Hamb 4E **47**
Chaloner Cres. SO45: Dib P 5E **53**
Chalvington Rd. SO53: Cha F........2E **15**
Chalybeate Cl. SO16: South 1F **29**
Chamberlain Hall SO16: Bass 5B **22**
Chamberlain Rd. SO17: South.......6C **22**
Chamberlayne Ct. SO52: N Bad ... 3F **13**
Chamberlayne Ho. SO31: Net A ... 1B **46**
Chamberlayne Leisure Cen. **4A 42**
Chamberlayne Rd. SO31: Burs......5F **43** .... (not continuous)
Chamberlayne Rd. SO31: Net A ...1A **46**
Chamberlayne Rd. SO50: E'leigh.....................................6A **16**
Chambers Av. SO51: Rom 5E **7**
Chambers Cl. SO16: Nur 4A **20**
Chancel Rd. SO31: Loc H 4F **49**
Chancery Ga. Bus. Cen. SO15: South...................................5C **28**
Chandlers Ct. SO14: South..................... 6E **5** (2C **40**) ....*(off Oriental Ter.)*
CHANDLER'S FORD 6G **9**
Chandler's Ford Ind. Est. SO53: Cha F................................. 2D **14**
Chandler's Ford Station (Rail).....1E **15**
Chandlers Ga. SO53: Cha F..........1E **15**
Chandlers Pl. SO31: Net A............1B **46**
Chandlers Way SO31: P Ga...........1F **49**
Chandos Ho. SO14: South..................... 5F **5** (2C **40**)
Chandos St. SO14: South..................... 5F **5** (2C **40**)
Channels Farm Rd. SO16: S'ing... 4F **23**
Channel Way SO14: South......................6H **5** (2D **40**)
Chantry, The PO14: Titch C 4G **49**
Chantry Hall SO14: South......................4G **5** (1D **40**) .... *(off Marsh La.)*
Chantry Rd. SO14: South....5H **5** (2D **40**)
Chantry Wlk. SO31: Net A 2C **46**

Compass Point S031: Hamb 5E **47**
Compass Way S031: Lwr Swan ...5A **44**
Compton Cl. S050: E'leigh 1H **15**
Compton Ho. S016: South............3F **29**
Compton Ho. S040: Tott............2C **26**
Compton Rd. S040: Tott............ 3G **27**
Compton Wlk.
 S014: South 1F **5** (6C **30**)
Concorde Cl. P015: Seg 2H **49**
Concorde Way P015: Seg 2H **49**
Condor Cl. S019: South............2F **41**
Conduct Gdns. S050: E'leigh 5G **15**
Conference Dr. S031: Loc H......4F **49**
Conifer Cl. S045: Hythe............3C **52**
Conifer Rd. S016: South............5E **21**
Coniston Gdns. S030: Hed E...... 6H **33**
Coniston Rd. S016: South............3A **28**
Coniston Rd. S050: E'leigh........ 5H **15**
Connemara Cres. P015: White.....6F **45**
Conrad Gdns. P015: White 5G **45**
Consort Cl. S050: E'leigh 2B **16**
Consort Rd. S050: E'leigh 2B **16**
Constable Cl. S019: South 3C **42**
Constantine Av. S053: Cha F 1H **15**
Constantine Cl. S053: Cha F 1H **15**
Consulate Ho.
 S014: South 6H **5** (2D **40**)
Conway Cl. S053: Cha F.............. 4D **14**
Cook Ho. S014: South 6G **5** (2D **40**)
 .... (off Royal Cres. Rd.)
Cooks La. S040: Calm 1B **26**
Cook St. S014: South 4F **5** (1C **40**)
Coombedale S031: Loc H............5F **49**
Cooper Rd. S040: A'hst.............2B **36**
Cooper's Cl. S018: W End 2C **32**
Coopers Ct. S014: South....6E **5** (2C **40**)
 ....(off Briton St.)
Cooper's La. S019: South............2F **41**
Copeland Rd. S016: South...........2B **28**
Copenhagen Towers
 S019: South 5G **41**
Copinger Cl. S040: Tott..............5C **26**
Copper Cl. S050: E'leigh............ 4H **15**
Copperfield Rd. S016: Bass.........4C **22**
Copperfields S040: Tott............4B **26**
Coppice Rd. S040: Calm 1C **26**
Coppice Gdns. S018: South 4D **32**
Copse, The S051: Rom................3F **7**
Copse, The S053: Cha F............. 2G **15**
Copse Bus. Cen. S040: Tott 1G **37**
Copse Cl. S021: Ott..................1C **10**
Copse Cl. S040: Tott.................5F **27**
Copse Cl. S052: N Bad................3C **12**
Copse La. S016: Chil...................6B **14**
Copse La. S031: Hamb...............5F **47**
Copse Rd. S018: South 1H **31**
Copse Vw. S019: South...............6E **33**
Copsewood Rd. S018: South 1G **31**
Copsewood Rd. S040: A'hst........2B **36**
Copsewood Rd. S045: Hythe........3C **52**
Copthorne La. S045: F'ley......... 2H **55**
Coracle Cl. S031: Wars 6D **48**
Corbiere Cl. S016: South............6C **20**
Corbould Rd. S045: Dib P............5C **52**
Cordelia Cl. S045: Dib...............3B **52**
Coriander Dr. S040: Tott............4B **26**
Coriander Way P015: White 5H **45**
Corinna Gdns. S045: Dib...........3B **52**
Corinthian Rd. S053: Cha F 6G **9**
Cork La. S040: March 3D **38**
Cormorant Dr. S045: Hythe....... 4G **53**
Cornel Rd. S019: South.............. 6H **31**
Cornfield Cl. S053: Cha F...........1B **14**
Cornflower Cl. S031: Loc H.........5C **48**
Cornforth Rd. S040: Calm...........2C **26**
Cornmarket S051: Rom...............5A **6**
Cornwall Cl. S018: South............1A **32**
Cornwall Cres. S018: South 1H **31**
Cornwall Rd. S018: South............ 1H **31**
Cornwall Rd. S053: Cha F 4E **15**
Coronation Av. S015: South.........6A **22**
Coronation Homes
 S018: South 3D **32**
Coronation Pde. S031: Hamb......4E **47**
 ....(off Kings Rd.)
Corsair Dr. S045: Dib.................3B **52**
Cortina Way S030: Hed E.............6B **34**

Corvette Av. S031: Wars 6D **48**
Corylus Ct. S040: Tott................2A **26**
Cosford Cl. S050: B'stke............5F **17**
Cossack Grn.
 S014: South 3F **5** (1C **40**)
Cosworth Dr. S018: Dib..............3A **52**
Cotsalls S050: Fair O.................2F **17**
Cotswold Cl. S045: Dib P...........4B **52**
Cotswold Rd. S016: South 3D **28**
Cotton Cl. S050: B'stke..............4E **17**
Coulsdon Rd. S030: Hed E.........5A **34**
Coultas Rd. S053: Cha F............ 4G **9**
COUNTESS MOUNTBATTEN
 HOUSE 1E **33**
COURSE PARK 5G **49**
Course Pk. Cres. P014: Titch C... 5G **49**
Court Cl. S018: South.................5A **32**
Court Cl. S040: Calm.................1C **26**
Courtenay Cl. P015: Seg............ 4H **49**
Court Ho. Cl. S045: Hythe..........2E **53**
Courtier Cl. S045: Dib...............3A **52**
Courtland Gdns. S016: Bass........4D **22**
Court Rd. S015: South 4B **30**
Court Royal M. S015: South........3B **30**
Coventry Rd. S015: South...........5B **30**
Covert, The S051: Rom...............5E **7**
Cowdray Cl. S016: South............5F **21**
Cowdray Cl. S050: B'stke...........5E **17**
Cowes La. S031: Wars................4B **50**
Cowley Cl. S016: South...............1C **28**
Cowper Rd. S019: South.............. 5D **32**
Cowslip Cl. S031: Loc H..............5C **48**
Cowslip Wlk. S040: Tott.............6C **26**
Cowslip Way S051: Rom...............4F **7**
Cox Dale P014: Titch C............. 6G **49**
COXFORD 1E **29**
Coxford Cl. S016: South.............1E **29**
Coxford Drove S016: South.........6E **21**
Coxford Rd. S016: South........... 1D **28**
Cox Row S053: Cha F.................4E **15**
Cox's Dr. S019: South................3B **42**
Cox's La. S019: South................3F **41**
Cozens Cl. S019: South............. 4G **41**
Crabapple Cl. S040: Tott............4B **26**
Crabbe Cl. S016: Bass................4C **22**
 .... (not continuous)
Crabbs Way S040: Tott...............4A **26**
Crableck La. S031: Sar G............2A **48**
Crabtree S016: South.................5C **30**
Crabwood Cl. S016: South.......... 1D **28**
Crabwood Dr. S030: W End.........2E **33**
Crabwood Rd. S016: South..........1C **28**
Cracknore Hard S040: March......4E **39**
Cracknore Hard La.
 S040: March 4E **39**
Cracknore Ind. Pk.
 S040: March 3G **39**
Cracknore Rd. S015: South 6H **29**
CRAMPMOOR 3H **7**
Crampmoor La. S051: Cram 3G **7**
Cranberry Cl. S040: March 4D **38**
Cranborne Gdns. S053: Cha F 4C **8**
Cranbourne Dr. S021: Ott..........2H **29**
Cranbourne Dr. S021: Ott............3B **10**
Cranbourne Pk. S030: Hed E 1A **44**
Cranbury, The S014: South.........5C **30**
 ....(off Cranbury Ter.)
Cranbury Av. S014: South..........5C **30**
Cranbury Cl. S021: Ott...............3B **10**
Cranbury Ct. S019: South............ 2H **41**
Cranbury Gdns. S031: Old N.......4F **43**
Cranbury Pl. S014: South...........5C **30**
Cranbury Rd. S019: South........... 2H **41**
Cranbury Rd. S050: E'leigh.........6A **16**
 .... (not continuous)
Cranbury Ter. S014: South..........5C **30**
Cranbury Towers S014: South.....5C **30**
 ....(off Cranbury Pl.)
Cranford Gdns. S053: Cha F 5C **8**
Cranford Rd. S017: South...........1C **30**
Cranford Way S017: South...........1C **30**
Cranleigh Ct. S017: South...........3C **30**
Cranleigh Rd. S030: Hed E.........5A **34**
Cranmer Dr. S016: Nur...............4A **20**
Cranmore S031: Net A................6C **42**
Cranwell Ct. S016: South........... 4D **20**

Craven Rd. S053: Cha F..............1F **15**
Craven St. S014: South 2F **5** (6C **30**)
Craven Wlk.
 S014: South 2E **5** (6C **30**)
Crawford Cl. S016: Nur...............4B **20**
Crawte Av. S045: Holb................5C **54**
Creedy Gdns. S018: W End.........6A **24**
Creighton Rd. S015: South......... 5D **28**
Crescent, The S019: South...........3A **42**
Crescent, The S031: Net A...........1B **46**
Crescent, The S040: March.........4C **38**
Crescent, The S050: E'leigh.........3A **16**
Crescent, The S051: Rom.............5E **7**
Crescent Rd. S031: Loc H........... 4D **48**
Cressey Rd. S051: Rom...............5B **6**
Crest Way S019: South...............1C **42**
Crestwood College
 Leisure Cen. 2H **15**
Crestwood Vw. S050: E'leigh 2H **15**
Crete Cotts. S045: Dib P............5C **52**
Crete La. S045: Dib P.................5C **52**
Crete Rd. S045: Dib P................5C **52**
Crichton Ho. S031: Net A 1B **46**
Crigdon Cl. S016: South.............3C **28**
Crispin Cl. S031: Loc H...............3F **49**
Crispin Cl. S050: Hor H.............. 3H **25**
Croft, The S040: Calm 1C **26**
Croft, The S050: E'leigh..............5A **16**
Croft, The S053: Cha F...............4E **15**
Croft Cl. S045: Hythe.................4E **53**
Crofton Cl. S017: South..............2C **30**
Crofton Way S031: Wars.............6A **48**
Cromalt Cl. S045: Dib P.............4A **52**
Cromarty Rd. S016: South...........4C **20**
Cromer Rd. S016: South.............2B **28**
Crompton Way P015: Seg........... 2G **49**
Cromwell Rd. S015: South...........4B **30**
Crooked Hays Cl. S040: March.... 4D **38**
Crookham Rd. S019: South......... 5H **41**
Crossbow Ho. S019: South..........3F **41**
 ....(off John Thornycroft Rd.)
CROSSHOUSE 5H **5** (2D **40**)
Cross Ho. Cen. S014: South 2E **41**
Crosshouse Rd.
 S014: South 6H **5** (2E **41**)
Crossley Ct. S015: South 5G **29**
Crossley Pl. S015: South.............5A **30**
Cross Rd. S019: South 4G **31**
Crosstrees S031: Sar G............... 1D **48**
Crossways, The S053: Cha F 3E **15**
Crosswell Cl. S019: South...........6C **32**
Crowders Grn. S021: Col C..........5F **11**
Crowlin Ho. S040: Tott...............3B **26**
Crown St. S015: South................3F **29**
Crows Nest La. S032: Botl 2D **34**
Crowsport S031: Hamb................4G **47**
CROWTHER 4G **47**
Crowther Cl. S019: South...........1C **42**
Croydon Cl. S016: South.............4A **20**
Crummock Rd. S053: Cha F.........6C **8**
Crusader Rd. S030: Hed E...........6B **34**
Crusaders Way S053: Cha F........1B **14**
Cuckmere La. S016: South..........3A **28**
CUCKOO BUSHES 5E **9**
Cuckoo La. S014: South....6D **4** (2B **40**)
Cudworth Mead S030: Hed E........2B **34**
Culford Av. S040: Tott................5F **27**
Culford Way S040: Tott...............5F **27**
Culver S031: Net A.....................6C **42**
Culver Cl. S016: South................1B **28**
Culvery Gdns. S018: W End........2A **32**
Cumberland Av. S053: Cha F...... 1G **15**
Cumberland Cl. S053: Cha F....... 1G **15**
Cumberland Pl.
 S015: South 1C **4** (6B **30**)
Cumberland St.
 S014: South 3G **5** (1D **40**)
Cumberland Way S045: Dib........3A **52**
Cumber Rd. S031: Loc H.............4C **48**
Cumbrian Way S016: South.........3C **28**
Cummins Grn. S031: Burs........... 4G **43**
Cunard Av. S015: South.............. 3G **29**
Cunard St. S014: South..............3C **40**
Cunningham Cres. S019: South....1B **42**
Cunningham Dr. S031: Loc H......3F **49**
Cunningham Gdns.
 S031: Old N 5F **43**

Cupernham La. S051: Rom...........1C **6**
Cupid Ho. S017: South...............6E **23**
CURBRIDGE 1H **45**
Curbridge Nature Reserve......... 1G **45**
CURDRIDGE 3H **35**
Curlew Cl. S016: South...............4F **21**
Curlew Cl. S045: Hythe...............4F **53**
Curlew Dr. S045: Hythe...............4F **53**
Curlew Sq. S050: E'leigh............ 5G **15**
Curlew Wlk. S045: Hythe.............4F **53**
Curzon Ct. S016: South.............. 5H **21**
Cutbush La. S018: South.............1A **32**
 .... (not continuous)
Cutforth Way S051: Rom.............2E **7**
Cutter Av. S031: Wars................6C **48**
Cygnus Gdns. S045: Dib.............3A **52**
Cypress Av. S019: South............. 6H **31**
Cypress Gdns. S040: Tott...........4B **26**
Cypress Gro. S053: Cha F............6E **9**
Cyprus Rd. P014: Titch C........... 6G **49**

D

Daffodil Rd. S016: S'ing..............5E **23**
Dahlia Rd. S016: Bass.................5C **22**
Daintree Cl. S019: South............ 2D **42**
Dairy La. S016: Nur................... 5G **19**
Daisy La. S031: Loc H.................4F **49**
Daisy Rd. S016: Bass................. 5D **22**
Dakota Way S050: E'leigh........... 1H **23**
Dale Grn. S053: Cha F.................5C **8**
Dale Rd. S016: South 1G **29**
Dale Rd. S045: Hythe.................3C **52**
Dales Way S040: Tott.................3B **26**
Dale Valley Cl. S016: South 1G **29**
Dale Valley Gdns. S016: South 1G **29**
Dale Valley Rd. S016: South 1G **29**
Dalmally Gdns. S018: South........ 3H **31**
Damen Cl. S030: Hed E.............. 6H **33**
Damson Cres. S050: Fair O.........6F **17**
Danebury Gdns. S053: Cha F......3C **14**
Danebury Way S016: Nur............6B **20**
Dane Cl. S031: Blac................... 5F **55**
Danehurst Rd. S031: Loc H.........5E **49**
Daniels Wlk. S040: Calm............2B **26**
Danube Dr. S031: Swanw........... 6F **45**
Dapple Pl. S040: March..............4E **39**
Dark La. S045: Blac................... 4E **55**
Darlee Ga. S031: Old N..............4F **43**
Darlington Gdns. S015: South ... 2H **29**
Dart Ho. S018: South................. 3H **31**
Dartington Rd. S050: B'stke 2D **16**
Dart Rd. S018: W End................6B **24**
Darwin Rd. S015: South............. 4H **29**
Darwin Rd. S050: E'leigh...........3B **16**
D Av. S045: F'ley......................2C **54**
David Lloyd Leisure
 Southampton 6B **20**
David Lloyd Leisure
 Southampton West End...........2F **33**
David Lockhart Ct.
 S017: South 2D **30**
David Moxon Annexe
 S014: South 4G **5** (1C **40**)
 .... (off St Mary's Pl.)
Davidson Cl. S045: Hythe............2F **53**
Dawlish Av. S015: South............. 3H **29**
Dawnay Cl. S016: S'ing...............4F **23**
Dawson Lodge S030: W End........2F **33**
Dawson Rd. S019: South.............3C **42**
Dawtrey Ct. S017: South.............1E **31**
Dayrell Cl. S040: Calm...............2B **26**
Deacon Cl. S019: South..............6A **32**
Deacon Cres. S019: South...........6A **32**
Deacon Rd. S031: Loc H..............5F **49**
Deacon Trad. Est.
 S050: E'leigh...........................5C **16**
Deakin Cl. S053: Cha F...............2E **15**
Dean Cl. S018: South................. 3G **31**
Dean Ct. S030: Hed E................. 4H **33**
Deanery, The S053: Cha F...........5C **8**
Deanery Halls
 S014: South 5G **5** (2D **40**)
 ....(off Marsh La.)

Deanfield Cl. S031: Hamb 5F 47	Dodwell Ter. S031: Burs............ 4H 43	Dunbar Cl. S016: South............... 4D 20	Edwin Jones Grn. S015: South 3A 30
Deanfields Ct. S018: South.......3B 32	Doe Wlk. S030: Hed E 3B 34	Duncan Cl. S019: South............... 4G 41	Effingham Gdns. S019: South.......1C 42
Dean M. S018: South 4A 32	Dolphin Cl. S050: B'stke 6E 17	Duncan Ct. S019: South..............6C 32	Ekless Ct. S031: Sar G 1D 48
Dean Pl. S053: Cha F 1E 15	Dolton Rd. S016: South................6D 20	Duncan Hood Ct. S017: South 6E 23	Elan Cl. S018: W End..................2B 32
Dean Rd. S018: South 3A 32	Dominy Cl. S045: Hythe 2F 53	Duncan Rd. S031: P Ga.................1F 49	Elderberry Cl. S050: Fair O 6G 17
Deansfield Cl. S051: Rom 4E 7	Doncaster Drove S050: E'leigh ...2G 23	Dundee Rd. S017: South...............2E 31	Elder Cl. S031: Loc H 5D 48
Dee Cl. S053: Cha F 2D 14	Doncaster Rd. S050: E'leigh 1A 24	Dundonald Cl. S019: South...........4F 41	Elder Cl. S040: March 4E 39
Deepdene, The S018: South.........3G 31	Donkey La. S031: Botl.................5E 35	Dundry Way S030: Hed E.............4A 34	Elder Grn. S021: Col C 5G 11
Deeping Cl. S019: South 4H 41	Donnington Dr. S053: Cha F 1E 15	Dunkirk Cl. S016: South...............5H 21	Eldon Ho. S014: South 5F 5 (2C 40)
Deerbrook Cl. S031: Sar G 2D 48	Donnington Gro. S017: South 1D 30	Dunkirk Rd. S016: South...............5G 21	Eldridge Gdns. S051: South..........4B 6
Deerhurst Cl. S040: Tott 5C 26	Dorchester Cl. S015: South.......3B 30	Dunnings La. S052: N Bad...........2C 12	Electron Way S053: Cha F 1E 15
Deerleap Cl. S045: Hythe 4E 53	Doric Cl. S053: Cha F 6H 9	Dunster Cl. S016: South...............4G 21	Elfin Cl. S031: South.....................3C 30
Deerleap Way S045: Hythe 4E 53	Dorland Gdns. S040: Tott............5C 26	Durban Cl. S031: Rom................4C 6	...............................(off Westwood Rd.)
Deer Pk. Farm Ind. Est.	Dormy Cl. S031: Sar G 4B 48	Durlston Rd. S016: South..............2B 28	Elgar Cl. S019: South....................2C 42
S050: Fair O............................2H 17	Dornan Ho. S014: South 4C 30	Durnford Rd. S014: South.............5D 30	Elgar Rd. S019: South....................2C 42
Deer Wlk. S030: Hed E..................3B 34	Dorrick Ct. S015: South 4B 30	Dutton La. S050: E'leigh..............3B 16	Elgin Cl. S045: Hythe....................4E 53
Defender Rd. S019: South.............2F 41	Dorrits, The S040: Tott...............4B 26	Duttons Rd. S051: Rom................4B 6	Elgin Cl. S015: South....................6H 29
Defender Wlk. S019: South..........2F 41	Dorset Rd. S053: Cha F 4E 15	Dyer Rd. S015: South...................4G 29	ELING...6H 27
Defoe Cl. P015: White 5G 45	Dorset St. S015: South................5C 30	Dymott Cl. S015: South 6H 29	Elingfield Ct. S040: Tott...............4G 27
De Grouchy La. S017: South.........2C 30	Dorval Ho. S015: South...............4A 30	Dyneley Grn. S018: South............2A 32	Elder Cl. S031: Loc H 4G 27
Delamere Gdns. S050: Fair O......4G 17	Dorval Mnr. S015: South.............4A 30	Dyram Cl. S050: E'leigh 2H 15	Eling La. S040: Tott......................4G 27
Delft Cl. S031: Loc H 4D 48	Douglas Cres. S019: South.........5C 32	Dyserth Cl. S019: South...............4B 42	Eling Sailing Club........................5H 27
Delius Av. S019: South 2D 42	Douglas Way S045: Hythe...........2C 52		Eling Tide Mill..............................5H 27
Dell, The S015: South....................5A 30	Dove Dale S050: E'leigh 5H 15		Eling Vw. S015: South...................4B 28
Dell Cl. S050: Fair O 2F 17	Dove Gdns. S031: P Ga 2F 49		Eling Wharf S040: Elin..................5H 27
Dell Rd. S018: South 1H 31	Dover St. S014: South..................4C 30	**E**	Eliot Cl. P015: White 4G 45
Delta Ho. S016: Chil 6G 13	Dowds Cl. S030: Hed E................3H 33		Eliot Ho. S017: South 1E 31
Dempsey Cl. S019: South.............1B 42	Downing Ct. P014: Titch C...........6G 49	Eagle Cl. S053: Cha F 3D 14	Elizabeth Cl. S030: W End...........2D 32
Denbigh Cl. S040: Tott.................6C 26	Downland Cl. S030: Botl..............4D 34	Earls Cl. S050: B'stke...................6F 17	Elizabeth Ct. S017: South.............2E 31
Denbigh Cl. S050: E'leigh............2H 15	Downland Cl. S031: Loc H 3E 49	Earl's Rd. S014: South 3C 30	Elizabeth Ct. S030: W End 2D 32
Denbigh Gdns. S016: Bass 5B 22	Downland Pl. S030: Hed E...........6H 33	East Bargate	Elizabeth Ct. S050: E'leigh...........3A 16
Dene Cl. S016: Chil 2B 22	Down La. S051: Rom 4E 7	S014: South 4E 5 (1C 40)	Elizabeth Gdns. S045: Dib P 5E 53
Dene Cl. S031: Sar G 3C 48	Downscroft Gdns.	Eastbourne Av. S015: South 3H 29	Elizabeth Way S050: E'leigh 2B 16
Dene Rd. S040: A'hst 3B 36	S030: Hed E 4H 33	Eastbrook Cl. S031: P Ga.............2E 49	Elkins Sq. S050: B'stke 6F 17
Dene Way S040: A'hst...................2B 36	Downside Av. S019: South...........5A 32	Eastchurch Cl. S016: South.........5D 20	Elland Cl. S050: Fair O 2F 17
Denham Flds. S050: Fair O 4G 17	Downs Pk. Av. S040: Elin............5G 27	Eastcot Cl. S045: Holb.................5B 54	Elldene Ct. S040: Tott..................6E 27
Denham Gdns. S031: Net A 2B 46	Downs Pk. Cres. S040: Elin 5G 27	East Dr. S050: B'stke...................3D 16	Elen Gdns. S053: Cha F 1C 14
Denmead Rd. S018: South...........3C 32	Downs Pk. Rd. S040: Elin 5G 27	Eastern Rd. S030: W End 2D 32	Elliot Cl. S040: Tott......................4C 26
Dennison Ct. S015: South...........3F 29	Downwood Cl. S045: Dib P.........4A 52	Eastfield Rd. S017: South.............3E 31	Elliot Ri. S030: Hed E...................2A 34
Denny Cl. S045: F'ley...................3H 55	Doyle Ct. S019: South..................4H 41	Eastgate St.	Ellis Rd. S019: South....................6E 33
Denyer Wlk. S019: South..............3E 41	Dragonfly Way S050: E'leigh 6C 10	S014: South 5E 5 (2C 40)	Ellwood Av. S019: South..............6E 33
Denzil Av. S014: South.................5C 30	Dragoon Cl. S019: South.............1C 42	East Horton Golf Cen. 2H 17	Ellwood Cl. S019: South...............6E 33
Denzil Av. S031: Net A 1B 46	Drake Cl. S031: Loc H 2F 49	East Horton Golf Course 2H 17	Elm Cl. S016: Bass.......................5B 22
Depden Gdns. S045: Dib P...........5B 52	Drake Cl. S040: March 3E 39	Eastlands Boatyard	Elm Ct. S019: South.....................2H 41
Depedene Cl. S045: Holb 4B 54	Drake Ho. S014: South......6G 5 (2D 40)	S031: Lwr Swan 4B 44	Elm Cres. S045: Hythe 1A 54
Derby Rd. S014: South.......1G 5 (6D 30)	..............................(off Royal Cres. Rd.)	EASTLEIGH 5B 16	Elmdale Cl. S031: Wars................6B 48
Derby Rd. S050: E'leigh 5G 15	Drake Rd. S050: B'stke................3E 17	Eastleigh Bus Station 4B 16	Elmes Dr. S015: South..................4D 28
Deridene Ct. S040: Tott................5C 26	Drakes Ct. S040: March...............2D 38	Eastleigh FC 2G 23	Elmfield Nth. Block
Derwent Cl. S018: W End.............2B 32	Drapers Copse Res. Pk.	Eastleigh Lakeside	S015: South 1A 4 (6H 29)
Derwent Dr. S040: Tott.................3B 26	S045: Dib.................................3A 52	Steam Railway 1H 23	Elmfield West Block
Derwent Rd. S016: South.............2C 28	Drayton Cl. S019: South...............5H 41	Eastleigh Mus. 5A 16	S015: South 2A 4 (6H 29)
Desborough Rd. S050: E'leigh 6A 16	Driftstone Gdns. S031: Loc H 3F 49	Eastleigh Rd. S050: Fair O 2F 17	Elm Gdns. S030: W End 6D 24
Devine Gdns. S050: B'stke...........5E 17	Driftwood Gdns. S040: Tott.........5B 26	Eastleigh Station (Rail) 4B 16	Elm Gro. S050: E'leigh..................5H 15
Devon Cl. S053: Cha F 4E 15	Drinkwater Cl. S050: E'leigh.......4H 15	Eastmeare Ct. S040: Tott............5C 26	Elmsleigh Cl. S016: Bass.............5C 22
Devon Dr. S053: Cha F 4E 15	Drive, The S030: W End 6B 24	East Pk.	Elmsleigh Gdns. S016: Bass.........5C 22
Devon M. S015: South...... 1A 4 (6A 30)	Drive, The S040: Tott...................6F 27	(Andrews Park)...............1E 5 (6C 30)	Elmslie Gdns. S031: Old N............4F 43
...............................(off Mandela Way)	Driveway, The S045: Blac.............4E 55	East Pk. Ter.	Elm St. S014: South 4H 5 (1D 40)
Devonshire Gdns. S031: Burs......3G 43	Droffatts Ho. S015: South...........4H 29	S014: South 1E 5 (6C 30)	Elm Ter. S014: South 5H 5 (2D 40)
Devonshire Gdns.	Drove, The S018: South................4A 32	East Rd. S040: March...................2E 39	Elmtree Cl. S040: A'hst.................3B 36
S045: Hythe................................6E 53	Drove, The S030: W End..............6F 25	East Rd. S045: Hard 6H 53	Elmtree Gdns. S051: Rom.............6F 7
Devonshire Mans.	Drove, The S040: Calm.................2B 26	East St. S014: South 4E 5 (1C 40)	Elmwood Ct. S016: South.............1F 29
S015: South 1C 4 (5B 30)	Drove, The S045: Blac..................4E 55	Eastville Rd. S050: Fair O 2F 17	Elsanta Cres. P014: Titch C..........6H 49
...............................(off Devonshire Rd.)	Drove Rd. S019: South.................6B 32	Eastwood Ct. S051: Rom.............5B 6	Elstree Rd. S019: South................4D 30
Devonshire Rd. S015: South........5B 30	Drummond Ct. S019: South 2G 41	Eaton Ho. S014: South.................5D 30	Elver Ct. S040: Elin......................5G 27
Dewar Cl. P015: Seg....................2G 49	Drummond Ct. S031: P Ga...........2B 16	...............................(off Radcliffe Rd.)	Embankment, The
Dew La. S050: E'leigh 4H 15	Drummond Dr. S014: South..........3E 31	Eddystone Rd. S040: Tott............1C 26	S015: South 6G 29
Dewsbury Ct. S018: South...........1A 32	Drummond Rd. P015: Seg............3H 49	Edelvale Rd. S018: South............2B 32	Embley Cl. S040: Calm.................1C 26
Dibben Wlk. S051: Rom................3F 7	Drummond Rd. S045: Hythe.........2E 53	Edenbridge Way S031: Sar G...... 1D 48	Embsay Rd. S031: Lwr Swan........5B 44
DIBDEN 1A 52	Drummond Way S053: Cha F 5C 8	Eden Rd. S018: W End..................6B 24	Emerald Cl. S019: South...............5B 32
Dibden Golf Course.....................2A 52	Drum Rd. S050: E'leigh 6F 33	Eden Wlk. S053: Cha F..................2D 14	Emerald Cres. S045: Hythe...........2F 53
DIBDEN PURLIEU 5B 52	Dryden Rd. S019: South...............6E 33	Edgehill Rd. S018: South..............2H 31	Emer Cl. S052: N Bad...................2E 13
Dibles Pk. S031: Wars..................6C 48	Duchess Ho. S019: South 3F 41	Edgehurst S031: Loc H 5D 48	Emily Davies Halls
Dibles Rd. S031: Wars..................6B 48	..............................(off John Thornycroft Rd.)	Edinburgh Ct. S015: South...........5E 29	S015: South 2C 4 (6B 30)
...............................(not continuous)	Duddon Cl. S018: W End...............2B 32	...............................(off Regent's Pk. Rd.)	...............................(off Fitzhugh St.)
Dibles Wharf S014: South.............6E 31	Duke Rd. S030: Hed E...................6B 34	Edith Haisman Cl.	Emmanuel Cl. P014: Titch C 5G 49
Dickens Dell S040: Tott................4A 26	Dukes Keep	S015: South 1A 4 (6H 29)	Emmett Rd. S016: Rown...............4D 20
Dickens Dr. P015: White 4G 45	S014: South.....................5G 5 (2D 40)	Edmunds Cl. S030: Botl...............6B 34	Emmons Cl. S031: Hamb...............5F 47
Didcot Rd. S015: South.................2G 29	...............................(off Duke St.)	Edney Path S031: Sar G 1B 48	Emperor Ho. S018: South..............4E 31
Diligence Cl. S031: Burs..............4G 43	Dukes Mill Cen. S051: Rom..........5B 6	Edward Av. S030: B'stke...............3D 16	Empire La. S015: South 1C 4 (6B 30)
Diment Cres. S051: South............2E 7	Duke St. S014: South 5G 5 (2D 40)	Edward Cl. S045: Blac..................5E 55	Empire Vw. S015: South 2C 4 (6B 30)
Dimond Cl. S018: South................2G 31	Dumas Dr. P015: White.................4G 45	Edward Rd. S015: South...............4G 29	Empress Pk. S014: South.............4D 30
Dimond Hill S018: South...............2G 31	Dumbleton Cl. S019: South.........6F 33	Edward Rd. S045: Hythe...............2E 53	Empress Rd. S014: South.............4D 30
Dimond Rd. S018: South...............1G 31	Dumbleton's Towers	Edwina Cl. S019: South................5H 31	Empress Rd. S015: South.............3F 29
Dingle Way S031: Loc H................3E 49	S019: South...............................1E 43	Edwina Cl. S052: N Bad...............3F 13	Endeavour Cl. S015: South...........4F 29
Dirty Dr. S052: N Bad 2H 13		Edwina Ho. S018: S'ing.................5G 23	Endeavour Cl. S031: Wars 6B 48
Disa Ho. S015: South 5A 30		Edwina Mountbatten Ho.	
Dodwell La. S031: Burs.................4H 43		S051: Rom 5B 6	
		...............................(off Broadwater Rd.)	

Endeavour Ct.
S014: South 6H **5** (2D **40**)
Enderwood Cl. S040: Tott 3B **26**
Endle St. S014: South 5H **5** (2E **41**)
Enfield Gro. S019: South 2G **41**
Englefield Rd. S018: South 4F **31**
English Rd. S015: South 4F **29**
Ennel Copse S052: N Bad 4E **13**
Ennerdale Gdns. S018: W End....2B **32**
Ennerdale Rd. S016: South 1C **28**
Ensign Pk. S031: Hamb 5E **47**
Ensign Way S031: Hamb 5E **47**
Enterprise Cl. S031: Wars...........6C **48**
Enterprise Rd. S016: Chil............ 6G **13**
Epping Cl. S018: South 2B **32**
Epsilon Ho. S016: Chil................ 6H **13**
Epsom Cl. P015: White.............. 5G **45**
...................................*(off Timor Cl.)*
Erica Cl. S031: Loc H 4D **48**
Eric Meadus Cl. S018: S'ing 5F **23**
Erskine Ct. S016: South 4D **20**
Escombe Rd. S050: B'stke..........4D **16**
Essex Grn. S053: Cha F 5E **15**
Estridge Cl. S031: Burs.............4G **43**
Ethelburt Av. S016: S'ing 4E **23**
Ethelred Gdns. S014: South 5C **26**
European Way S014: South 3D **40**
Evans St. S014: South........ 4F **5** (1C **40**)
Evelyn Cres. S015: South............3H **29**
Evenlode Rd. S016: South...........2C **28**
Evergreen Cl. S040: March 4D **38**
Evergreens S040: Elin................5G **27**
Evesham Cl. S016: Bass 4D **22**
Ewart Ct. S045: Hythe................2E **53**
Ewell Way S040: Tott.................. 2C **26**
Exbury Cl. S050: B'stke..............5E **17**
Exbury Rd. S045: Blac 5E **55**
Exeter Cl. S018: South 2A **32**
Exeter Cl. S031: Loc H 4D **48**
Exeter Cl. S050: E'leigh...............2H **15**
Exeter Rd. S018: South...............3A **32**
Exford Av. S018: South 4C **32**
Exford Dr. S018: South 4C **32**
Exleigh Cl. S018: South..............5B **32**
Exmoor Cl. P015: White..............6F **45**
Exmoor Cl. S040: Tott.................4B **26**
Exmoor Rd. S014: South 5D **30**
Exmouth St.
S014: South 2E **5** (6C **30**)
Eyeworth Wlk. S045: Dib 3A **52**
Eynham Av. S019: South.............5C **32**
Eynham Cl. S019: South..............5C **32**
Eynham Gdns. S019: South 5B **32**

F

Faber M. S051: Rom 4E **7**
Factory Rd. S050: E'leigh............5A **16**
Fairbairn Wlk. S053: Cha F.........1B **14**
Fairbourne Ct. S019: South..........3E **41**
Faircross Cl. S045: Holb 5B **54**
Fairfax Ct. S019: South...............5E **33**
Fairfax M. S019: South................5E **33**
Fair Fld. S051: Rom......................4C **6**
Fairfield Lodge S016: South 5G **21**
Fairfield Rd. S021: Shaw 1D **10**
Fair Grn. S019: South..................6B **32**
Fairholme Cl. S050: E'leigh..........4A **16**
Fairlawn Cl. S016: Rown............. 3D **20**
Fairlawns S031: Burr 4F **45**
Fairlea Grange S016: Bass 5B **22**
Fairlie Cl. S030: Hed E 1A **34**
Fairmead Cl. S031: Wars 6C **48**
Fairmead Way S040: Tott............6E **27**
FAIR OAK 6G **17**
Fair Oak Ct. S050: Fair O 2F **17**
Fair Oak Rd. S050: B'stke 4D **16**
Fair Oak Rd. S050: Fair O 4D **16**
Fair Oak Squash Club 1F **17**
Fairthorne Manor Golf Course 6G **35**
Fairview Cl. S045: Hythe..............3E **53**
Fairview Cl. S051: Rom.................4E **7**
Fairview Dr. S019: South 4E **7**
Fairview Pde. S045: Hythe 4E **53**
Fairway, The S031: Wars 6D **48**
Fairway Gdns. S016: Rown...........4C **20**

Fairway Rd. S045: Hythe..............3C **52**
Falaise Cl. S016: South 5G **21**
Falconer Ct. S045: Hard...............2B **54**
Falcon Flds. S045: F'ley...............2H **55**
Falcon Sq. S050: E'leigh 6G **15**
Falcon Way S032: Botl.................2D **34**
Falkland Cl. S053: Cha F 4E **15**
Falkland Rd. S015: South 3E **29**
Falkland Rd. S053: Cha F 5E **15**
Fallow Cres. S030: Hed E............3B **34**
Fanshawe St. S014: South...........5C **30**
FAREHAM COMMUNITY
HOSPITAL 2E **49**
Faringdon Rd. S018: South 4D **32**
Farley Cl. S050: Fair O 2G **17**
Farley Cl. S018: South 1H **29**
Farm Cl. S031: Hamb 5G **47**
Farm Cl. S040: Calm 1B **26**
Farm Cl. S018: S'ing 5F **23**
Farm La. S040: A'hst 3B **36**
Farm Rd. P014: Titch..................5H **49**
Farrell Flds. S040: March.............3D **38**
Farringford Rd. S019: South 5D **32**
Farthings, The P014: Titch C 1G **51**
Fastnet Cl. S016: South...............4C **20**
FAWLEY 2H **55**
Fawley Bus. Cen. S045: F'ley.......3G **55**
Fawley By-Pass S045: F'ley 3H **55**
Fawley Rd. S015: South...............5E **29**
Fawley Rd. S045: F'ley.................2E **55**
Fawley Rd. S045: Hard.................4E **53**
Fawley Rd. S045: Hythe...............4E **53**
Fawley Rd. S045: Hythe...............6F **53**
Fawn Cres. S030: Hed E 3B **34**
Fell Cl. S031: Loc H 3E **49**
Feltham Cl. S051: Rom 4F **7**
Felton Cl. S031: Net A..................1C **46**
Fenwick Ho. S014: South.............5E **31**
...................................*(off Meridian Way)*
Fernacre Bus. Pk. S051: Rom.......3A **6**
Fern Cl. S019: South 5F **33**
Ferndale Rd. S040: March 4D **38**
Ferndene Way S018: South..........3H **31**
Fernhill S053: Cha F 1G **15**
Fernhills Rd. S045: Hythe 5F **53**
Fernhurst Cl. S021: Col C.............4F **11**
Fernlea Gdns. S016: Bass............6A **22**
Fernlea Way S045: Dib P.............4B **52**
Fern Rd. S019: South 3H **41**
Fern Rd. S045: Hythe 3C **52**
Fernside Cl. S016: South 3D **28**
Fernside Cl. S045: Holb...............5A **22**
Fernside Ct. S016: Bass..............5A **22**
Fernside Wlk. S050: Fair O 1G **17**
Fernside Way S050: Fair O.......... 1G **17**
Fern Way P015: Seg 4H **49**
Fernwood Cres. S018: South 3H **31**
Fernyhurst Av. S016: Rown.......... 4D **20**
Ferrybridge Grn. S030: Hed E......5A **34**
Ferrymans Quay S031: Net A.......2A **46**
Field Cl. S016: S'ing.....................4E **23**
Field Cl. S031: Loc H...................5E **49**
Fielden Cl. S052: N Bad 3C **12**
Fielders Ct. S030: W End 2E **33**
Fieldfare Ct. S040: Tott................3B **26**
Fielding Rd. P015: White.............4G **45**
Fields Cl. S045: Blac 4E **55**
Field Vw. S053: Cha F 1B **14**
Filton Cl. S040: Calm...................2B **26**
Finches, The S016: South 3F **29**
Finches, The S017: South 1D **30**
Finches Cl. S021: Col C............... 5G **11**
Finlay Cl. S019: South..................1C **42**
Finley Cl. S040: Calm...................2A **26**
Finzi Cl. S019: South....................2C **42**
Fircroft Dr. S053: Cha F 2F **15**
Firecracker Cl. S031: Sar G.........4C **48**
Firecrest Cl. S016: South.............4F **21**
Firgrove Cl. S015: South.............. 4G **29**
Firgrove Rd. S015: South............. 4G **29**
Fir Rd. S040: A'hst......................3A **36**
Firs, The S016: Bass 5B **22**
Firs Dr. S030: Hed E....................5H **33**
First Av. S015: South...................4B **28**
First St. S045: Hard.....................6E **53**
Fir Tree Cl. S018: South 3B **32**
Firtree Gro. S045: Hythe 6E **53**

Fir Tree La. S050: Hor H.............. 1G **25**
Firtree Way S019: South 6B **32**
Firwood Cl. S053: Cha F 5E **9**
Fisher's Rd. S040: Elin................5G **27**
Fishlake Mdws. S051: Rom 3B **6**
Fitzgerald Cl. P015: White............5G **45**
FITZHUGH 4B **30**
Fitzhugh Pl. S015: South..............4B **30**
Fitzhugh St.
S015: South 2C **4** (6B **30**)
Fitzroy Cl. S016: Bass.................2B **22**
Five Elms Dr. S051: Rom..............5E **7**
Flamborough Cl. S016: South.......6B **20**
Flanders Fld. La. S016: South.......3A **28**
Flanders Ind. Pk. S030: Hed E 3H **33**
Flanders Rd. S030: Hed E 3H **33**
FLEETEND 6D **48**
Fleet End Rd. S031: Wars 6D **48**
Fleet Ter. S021: Ott......................4A **10**
Fleming Av. S052: N Bad 4E **13**
Fleming Cl. P015: Seg..................3H **49**
Fleming Cl. S052: N Bad 4F **13**
Fleming Ho. S050: E'leigh............ 5G **15**
Fleming Pl. S021: Col C 4F **11**
Fleming Pl. S051: Rom.................5B **6**
Fleming Rd. S016: S'ing 5F **23**
Fletcher Cl. S045: Dib.................3A **52**
Fletchwood La. S040: A'hst...........3A **36**
...............................*(not continuous)*
Fletchwood La. S040: Tott...........3A **36**
...............................*(not continuous)*
Fletchwood Meadows
Nature Reserve 2B **36**
Fletchwood Rd. S040: Tott 5B **26**
Fleuret Cl. S045: Hythe................6E **53**
FLEXFORD 6B **8**
Flexford Cl. S053: Cha F 4B **8**
Flexford Nature Reserve..............5C **8**
Flexford Rd. S052: N Bad............ 1G **13**
Flint Cl. S019: South.....................1E **43**
Floating Bri. Rd.
S014: South 6H **5** (2E **41**)
Florence Rd. S019: South 3F **41**
Florins, The P014: Titch C 6H **49**
Flowerdown Cl. S040: Calm 3B **26**
Flowers Cl. S031: Hamb...............4E **47**
Folland Cl. S021: Col C.................3E **13**
Font Cl. P014: Titch C 4G **49**
Fontwell Cl. S040: Calm...............2C **26**
Foord Rd. S030: Hed E................ 6G **33**
Footner Cl. S051: Rom.................2F **7**
Forbes Cl. S016: South 3D **20**
Ford Av. S053: Cha F 3F **15**
Fordington Rd. S053: Cha F..........1E **15**
Forest Cl. S052: N Bad 2C **12**
Forest Cl. S053: Cha F 5E **9**
Forest Edge S045: F'ley.............. 2G **55**
Forest Education Centre
Pupil Referral Unit 3A **52**
Foresters Rd. S045: F'ley.............4F **55**
Forest Ga. S045: Blac..................5F **55**
Forest Hills Dr. S018: South......... 6G **23**
Forest Hill Way S045: Dib P.........4C **52**
Forest La. S045: Hard..................2B **54**
Forest Mdw. S045: Hythe.............6E **53**
Forest Rd. S053: Cha F 5F **9**
Forest Vw. S014: South.....5D **4** (1B **40**)
Forest Way S040: Calm...............1A **26**
Forge Cl. S031: Burs...................4G **43**
Forge La. S045: F'ley...................3H **55**
Forster Rd. S014: South...............4C **30**
Forsythia Cl. S030: Hed E............3H **33**
Forsythia Cl. S045: Hythe............1A **54**
Forsythia Pl. S019: South............ 6H **31**
Forth Cl. S053: Cha F 2D **14**
Forth Ho. S014: South..................5E **31**
Fort Rd. S019: South 2G **41**
Fortune Ct. S053: Cha F 1E **15**
Foster Way S051: Rom..................2E **7**
Foundry Cl. S019: South...............3F **41**
Foundry Cres. S031: Burs.............5F **43**
Foundry La. S015: South..............3F **29**
Fountain Cl. S021: Col C...............4F **11**
Fountain Ct. S030: Hed E.............5H **33**
Fountains Pk. S031: Net A............6A **42**
Four Acres S030: Botl..................5E **35**
FOURPOSTS 1A **4** (6A **30**)

Fourposts Hill
S015: South 1A **4** (6A **30**)
Fourshells Cl. S045: F'ley.............4F **55**
Fowey, The S045: Blac.................3E **55**
Fowlers Rd. S030: Hed E 3H **33**
Fowlers Wlk. S016: Chil...............5H **13**
Foxbury Cl. S045: Hythe 4E **53**
Fox Cl. S050: B'stke....................6E **17**
Foxcott Cl. S019: South...............5H **41**
Foxcroft Dr. S045: Holb................5B **54**
Foxfield S031: P Ga......................1F **49**
Foxglade S045: Blac 5F **55**
Foxgloves, The S030: Hed E 6B **34**
Foxhayes La. S045: Blac..............5F **55**
Foxhills S040: A'hst.....................1C **36**
FOXHILLS 1C **36**
Foxhills Cl. S040: A'hst................2B **36**
Foxlands S045: Blac 5F **55**
Fox's Wlk. S045: Blac..................5F **55**
Foxtail Dr. S045: Dib P.................5C **52**
Foxy Paddock S045: Blac 5F **55**
Foyes Ct. S015: South.................4H **29**
Foy Gdns. S031: Wars 6A **48**
Foyle Rd. S053: Cha F 1D **14**
Fragorum Flds. P014: Titch C 5G **49**
Frampton Cl. S021: Col C.............4F **11**
Frampton Way S040: Tott.............5F **27**
Francis Copse S021: Col C 4G **11**
Franconia Dr. S016: Nur.............. 6H **19**
Frankie's Fun Factory..................4B **6**
Franklyn Av. S019: South.............1A **42**
Fraser Cl. S016: South 3D **20**
Fratton Way S050: Fair O.............2F **17**
Fraylea S045: Dib P.....................5E **53**
Freda Routh Gdns.
S050: Fair O........................... 2G **17**
Frederick St. S014: South............ 5D **30**
Freegrounds Av. S030: Hed E.......5A **34**
Freegrounds Cl. S030: Hed E.......6A **34**
Freegrounds Rd. S030: Hed E.......5A **34**
FREEMANTLE 5G **29**
Freemantle Bus. Cen.
S015: South 6G **29**
Freemantle Cl. S019: South 6H **31**
Freemantle Comn. Rd.
S019: South 6H **31**
Freemantle Rd. S051: Rom............2E **7**
French Ct. S014: South.....6D **4** (2B **40**)
...................................*(off Castle Way)*
French St. S014: South.....6D **4** (2B **40**)
Frensham Cl. S030: Hed E............5A **34**
Frensham Ct. S030: Hed E 5A **34**
Freshfield Rd. S015: South 4F **29**
Freshfield Sq. S015: South 4F **29**
Freshwater Ct. S053: Cha F..........5G **9**
Friars Cft. S031: Net A..................6B **42**
Friars Cft. S040: Calm..................1B **26**
Friars Rd. S050: E'leigh................6H **15**
Friars Way S018: S'ing 5F **23**
Fritham Cl. S040: Tott..................4C **26**
Fritham Rd. S018: South 3D **32**
Frobisher Cl. S040: March 2E **39**
Frobisher Gdns. S019: South........1C **42**
Frobisher Ind. Cen. S051: Rom......4A **6**
Froghall S045: Dib P....................5E **53**
Frogmore La. S016: Nur...............6B **20**
Frome Cl. S040: March 4E **39**
Frome Rd. S018: W End 6A **24**
Frost La. S045: Hythe..................5E **53**
FROSTLANE 5G **53**
Fry Cl. S031: Hamb......................3G **47**
Fry Cl. S045: F'ley........................3F **55**
Fryern Arc. S053: Cha F 6F **9**
Fryern Cl. S053: Cha F................ 1G **15**
FRYERN HILL 1F **15**
Fuchsia Gdns. S016: South.......... 1H **29**
Fulcrum P015: White.................... 6H **45**
Fulford Rd. S052: N Bad..............3E **13**
Fullerton Cl. S019: South 5H **41**
Fullerton Pl. S017: South............. 3D **30**
Fulmar Cl. S016: South 4F **21**
Fulmar Dr. S045: Hythe................4F **53**
Furze Cl. S019: South..................6A **32**
Furzedale Gdns. S045: Hythe.......5F **53**
Furzedale Pk. S045: Hythe...........5F **53**
Furzedown M. S045: Hythe...........5F **53**
Furzedown Rd. S017: South 1C **30**

Furze Dr. S051: Rom 2E **7**
Furze Rd. S019: South 6A **32**
Furzey Av. S045: Hythe 4F **53**
Furzey Cl. S045: F'ley 4F **55**
Fyeford Cl. S016: Rown............. 3D **20**
Fyfield Cl. P015: White............. 5G **45**

G

Gables Ct. S016: Bass..................4B **22**
Gage Cl. S040: March.................3E **39**
Gainsborough Cl. S019: South.....3C **42**
Gainsborough Ct. S052: N Bad.....3F **13**
Gainsford Rd. S019: South...........6F **31**
Gala Bingo Southampton 5D **20**
Galleon Cl. S031: Wars 6D **48**
Gallops, The P014: Titch C......... 5H **49**
Galsworthy Rd. S040: Tott...........4C **26**
Gamble Cl. S019: South 1H **41**
Gamma Ho. S016: Chil 6G **13**
Gammon Cl. S030: Hed E.............1H **33**
Ganger Farm La. S051: Rom..........2F **7**
Ganger Rd. S051: Rom.................3F **7**
Gang Warily Recreation
& Community Cen. 3E **55**
Gannet Cl. S016: South 4F **21**
Gannet Cl. S045: Hythe 4F **53**
Gantry Ct. S015: South........2C **4** (6B **30**)
..................(off Blechynden Ter.)
Garden M. S031: Wars 6A **48**
Gardiner Cl. S040: March.............3E **39**
Garfield Rd. S019: South.............4G **31**
Garfield Rd. S031: Net A.............1A **46**
Garland Way S040: Tott...............3B **26**
Garnier Dr. S050: B'stke.............2C **16**
..................(not continuous)
Garnock Rd. S019: South.............3F **41**
Garratt Cl. S030: Hed E..............1A **34**
Garretts Cl. S019: South 4A **42**
Garrick Gdns. S019: South 3A **42**
Garth, The S045: Dib P...............5C **52**
Garton Rd. S019: South...............2G **41**
Gashouse Hill S031: Net A...........2C **46**
Gaston Gdns. S051: Rom..............4B **6**
Gatcombe S031: Net A 6C **42**
Gatcombe Gdns. S018: W End......1A **32**
Gatehouse, The S018: South........ 3G **31**
Gatehouse, The S030: W End........1C **32**
Gateley Hall S015: South 4B **30**
Gaters Hill S018: W End...............6A **24**
Gatwick Cl. S016: South 5E **21**
Gavan St. S019: South 6D **32**
Gemini Cl. S016: South 5D **20**
Gento Cl. S030: Botl....................5C **34**
George Curl Way
S018: S'ton A............................. 3H **23**
George Perrett Way
S053: Cha F.................................3B **14**
George Raymond Rd.
S050: E'leigh............................. 5H **15**
George St. S050: E'leigh 4B **16**
Georges Way S050: E'leigh 4G **15**
George Wright Cl.
S050: E'leigh............................. 5H **15**
Georgina Cl. S040: Tott................2A **26**
Gerard Cres. S019: South.............5D **32**
Gibbs Cl. S045: Hythe 6E **53**
Gibbs Rd. S014: South 2D **4** (6B **30**)
Gilbury Cl. S018: S'ing 5G **23**
Gilchrist Gdns. S031: Wars.........2A **50**
Giles Cl. S030: Hed E 2B **34**
Gillcrest P014: Titch C.................3G **49**
Gilman Cl. S050: B'stke...............3D **16**
Gilpin Cl. S019: South 6E **33**
Gipsy Gro. S015: South 4G **29**
Girton Cl. P014: Titch C...............6G **49**
Glade, The S045: Blac..................5E **55**
Glade, The S053: Cha F...............4H **9**
Glades, The S031: Loc H..............3E **49**
Gladstone Ho.
S014: South.......................2G **5** (6D **30**)
..................(off Golden Gro.)
Gladstone Rd. S019: South...........6B **32**
Glasslaw Rd. S018: South.............3A **32**
Glebe Ct. S017: South 1C **30**
Glebe Ct. S030: Botl....................4E **35**
Glebe Ct. S050: Fair O.................1G **17**

Glebe Rd. S014: South 5H **5** (2D **40**)
Glen, The S050: E'leigh 5A **16**
..................(off Grantham Rd.)
Glencarron Way S016: Bass..........6A **22**
Glencoyne Gdns. S016: South 1D **28**
Glenda Cl. S031: Wars 1A **50**
Glendale S031: Loc H...................5E **49**
Glendowan Rd. S053: Cha F........6B **8**
Gleneagles Equestrian Cen. 4D **24**
Glen Eyre Cl. S016: Bass..............5C **22**
Glen Eyre Dr. S016: Bass 4C **22**
Glen Eyre Halls S016: Bass...........4C **22**
Glenfield Av. S018: South 4H **31**
Glenfield Cres. S018: South 4H **31**
Glenfield Way S018: South 4H **31**
Glenlea Cl. S030: W End 2D **32**
Glenlea Dr. S030: W End 2D **32**
Glen Lee S018: South 3A **32**
Glenmore Ct. S017: South...........3D **30**
Glenn Rd. S030: W End................1D **32**
Glen Pk. Mobile Home Pk.
S021: Col C................................. 5G **11**
Glen Rd. S019: South 4F **41**
Glen Rd. S031: Sar G...................6C **44**
..................(not continuous)
Glen Rd. S031: Swanw...............6C **44**
..................(not continuous)
Glenside S030: W End..................2D **32**
Glenside S045: Hythe 3C **52**
Glenside Av. S019: South 1D **42**
Glenwood Av. S016: Bass 4C **22**
Glenwood Ct. S050: Fair O.......... 1H **17**
Gloster Ct. P015: Seg..................2G **49**
Gloucester Dr. S031: Sar G..........2E **49**
Gloucester Sq.
S014: South.......................6E **5** (2C **40**)
..................(off High St.)
Glyn Jones Cl. S045: F'ley...........4F **55**
Goals Soccer Cen.
Southampton 5E **29**
Godfrey Olson Ho.
S050: E'leigh.............................4B **16**
God's House Tower 6E **5** (3C **40**)
Goldcrest Gdns. S016: South........4E **21**
Goldcrest La. S040: Tott..............3B **26**
Golden Ct. S030: W End...............6F **25**
Golden Gro. S014: South......2G **5** (6D **30**)
Golden Hind Pk. S045: Hythe.......4C **52**
Goldsmith Cl. S040: Tott............4C **26**
Goldsmith Rd. S050: E'leigh 6H **15**
Goldsmiths Ct.
S014: South.......................6E **5** (2C **40**)
..................(off Briton St.)
Goldwire Dr. S053: Cha F............2B **14**
Golf Course Rd. S016: Bass..........4A **22**
Goodacre Dr. S053: Cha F............2B **14**
Goodalls La. S030: Hed E............. 4H **33**
Goodison Cl. S050: Fair O............ 6G **17**
Goodlands Va. S030: Hed E 4G **33**
Goodwin Cl. S016: South 1B **28**
Goodwood P014: Titch C.............. 5H **49**
Goodwood Gdns. S016: South 3C **26**
Goodwood Rd. S050: E'leigh........ 2G **15**
Gordon Av. S014: South................3C **30**
Gordon Rd. S053: Cha F..............4F **9**
Gordon Ter. S019: South..............3A **42**
Gorse Cl. S031: Loc H 5D **48**
Gorselands Rd. S018: South.........2B **32**
Gort Cres. S019: South 1B **42**
Gover Rd. S016: South.................2A **28**
Grace Dieu Gdns. S031: Burs 4F **43**
Graddidge Way S040: Tott...........4C **26**
Grafton Gdns. S016: South...........4G **21**
Graham Cl. S019: South...............5A **32**
Graham Ho. S014: South.............5E **31**
Graham Rd. S014: South..............5C **30**
Graham St. S014: South...............5E **31**
Grainger Gdns. S019: South..........2C **42**
Granada Rd. S030: Hed E.............6G **33**
Granary La. S050: E'leigh 4A **16**
Granby Gro. S017: South..............6D **22**
Grange Cl. S018: S'ing 5G **23**
Grange Cl. S031: S'ing 6A **44**
Grange Ct. S031: Net A................1A **46**
Grange Dr. S021: Ott...................5B **10**

Grange Dr. S030: Hed E 4B **34**
Grange Dr. S050: E'leigh 5B **10**
Grange Farm S031: Net A 6B **42**
Grange M. S051: Rom...................3F **7**
Grange Pk. S030: Hed E...............2A **34**
Grange Rd. S016: South................2F **29**
Grange Rd. S030: Botl..................3A **34**
Grange Rd. S030: Hed E 3A **34**
Grange Rd. S031: Net A 1A **46**
Grangewood Ct. S050: Fair O 5G **17**
Grangewood Gdns.
S050: Fair O............................... 6G **17**
Grantham Av. S031: Hamb............4E **47**
Grantham Rd. S019: South 5H **31**
Grantham Rd. S050: E'leigh......... 5H **15**
Granville St.
S014: South.......................4H **5** (1D **40**)
Grasdean Cl. S018: South 2A **32**
Grasmere S050: E'leigh............... 5H **15**
Grasmere Cl. S018: W End...........2B **32**
Grasmere Ct. S016: South 1C **28**
Grassymead P014: Titch C........... 3G **49**
Grateley Cl. S019: South 5H **41**
Gravel Wlk. S045: F'ley...............4F **55**
Gray Cl. S031: Wars 5D **48**
Grayling Mead S051: Rom............4B **6**
Graylings S015: South 3E **29**
Grays Av. S045: Hythe 3F **53**
Grays Cl. S021: Col C..................5F **11**
Greatbridge Rd. S051: Rom..........1A **6**
Gt. Elms Cl. S045: Holb 5B **54**
Gt. Farm Rd. S050: E'leigh 4H **15**
Gt. Well Dr. S051: Rom................5C **6**
Greatwood Cl. S045: Hythe..........4E **53**
Green, The S031: Sar G...............1C **48**
Green, The S051: Rom..................3F **7**
Greenacres Rd. S021: Ott.............2C **10**
Greenacres Rd. S031: Loc H..........4C **48**
Greenacres Rd. S031: Sar G..........4C **48**
Greenaway La. S031: Wars...........5B **48**
Greenbank Cres. S016: Bass 4B **22**
Green Cl. S045: Hythe 3E **53**
Greendale Cl. S053: Cha F........... 1G **15**
Greenfield Cl. S030: Hed E 1H **43**
Greenfields Av. S040: Tott 2E **27**
Greenfields Cl. S040: Tott............2E **27**
Greenfinch Cl. S050: E'leigh......... 6F **15**
Greenhill La. S016: Rown 1C **20**
Greenhill Ter. S051: Rom..............5A **6**
Greenhill Vw. S051: Rom..............5A **6**
Greenlands Vw. S030: Botl...........4C **34**
Green La. S045: Blac
Roughdown La......................5B **54**
Green La. S045: Blac
Walker's La. Nth.....................5F **55**
Green La. S016: Chil 6B **14**
Green La. S016: South 1C **28**
Green La. S031: Burr 4E **45**
Green La. S031: Burs 3F **43**
Green La. S031: Hamb 5G **47**
Green La. S031: Lwr Swan...........5B **44**
Green La. S031: Old N.................3F **43**
Green La. S031: Wars 6D **48**
Green La. S040: Calm 5B **18**
Green La. S051: Ampf..................4H **7**
Green La. S051: Rom...................4H **7**
Greenlea Cres. S016: S'ing..........4F **23**
Green Pk. Rd. S016: South............4C **28**
Greenridge Ct. S015: South 3B **30**
..................(off Marshall Sq.)
Greenway Ct. S016: South 1G **29**
Greenways S016: S'ing.................4F **23**
Greenways S053: Cha F................ 1G **15**
Greenwich, The
S014: South.......................6E **5** (2C **40**)
..................(off High St.)
Greenwich, The S045: Blac..........4E **55**
Greenwood Av. S016: Rown..........3B **20**
Greenwood Cl. S050: E'leigh........ 6H **15**
Greenwood Cl. S051: Rom............5C **6**
Gregory Gdns. S040: Calm...........2C **26**
Grenadier Cl. S031: Loc H............5F **49**
Grendon Cl. S016: Bass 4D **22**
Grenville Cl. S015: South 4A **30**
Grenville Cl. S018: South 6H **23**
Grenville Gdns. S045: Dib P..........6E **53**
Gresley Gdns. S030: Hed E 1A **34**

Greville Rd. S015: South 4H **29**
Greyhound Cl. S030: Hed E........... 6H **25**
Greywell Av. S016: South 5G **21**
Greywell Ct. S016: South 5G **21**
Griffen Cl. S050: B'stke................5E **17**
Griffin Ct. S017: South 3E **31**
Griffon Cl. S031: Burs 4G **43**
Grosvenor Cl. S017: South............1E **31**
Grosvenor Ct. S017: South............2E **31**
..................(off Grosvenor Rd.)
Grosvenor Gdns. S017: South.......1E **31**
Grosvenor Cl. S030: W End.......... 3D **32**
Grosvenor Mans. S015: South.......5B **30**
..................(off Devonshire Rd.)
Grosvenor M. S017: South............1E **31**
Grosvenor Rd. S017: South............1E **31**
Grosvenor Rd. S053: Cha F 4G **9**
Grosvenor Sq. S015: South...........5B **30**
Grove, The S019: South................4B **42**
Grove, The S031: Burs 4G **43**
Grove, The S031: Net A................6D **42**
Grovebury S031: Loc H 5E **49**
Grove Bus. Pk. S051: Rom...........4A **6**
Grove Copse S019: South.............4C **42**
Grove Gdns. S019: South...............4B **42**
Grovely Way S051: Cram 3H **7**
Grove M. S019: South 3B **42**
Grove Pl. S019: South 3B **42**
Grove Rd. S015: South 4G **29**
Grove Rd. S021: Shaw 1C **10**
Grove St. S014: South 4G **5** (1D **40**)
Guardian Ct. S017: South 2C **30**
Guernsey Cl. S016: South..............6C **20**
Guest Rd. S050: B'stke 4D **16**
Guildford Dr. S053: Cha F 4D **14**
Guildford St.
S014: South.......................1H **5** (6D **30**)
Guildhall Pl.
S014: South.......................2D **4** (6B **30**)
..................(off Guildhall Sq.)
Guildhall Sq.
S014: South.......................2D **4** (6B **30**)
..................(off Oriental Ter.)
Guild Ho. S014: South 6E **5** (2C **40**)
Guillemot Cl. S045: Hythe 4F **53**
Gull Coppice P015: White............ 6G **45**
Gulls, The S040: March 3D **38**
Gullycroft Mead S030: Hed E....... 4H **33**
Gurney Rd. S015: South 3G **29**
Gwelo Dr. S030: Hed E 1H **43**

H

Hack Dr. S021: Col C...................5F **11**
Hackworth Gdns. S030: Hed E 1A **34**
Haddon Dr. S050: E'leigh 2A **16**
Hadleigh Gdns. S050: E'leigh........2A **16**
Hadley Fld. S045: Hard 3B **54**
Hadrians Cl. S053: Cha F 6G **9**
Hadrian Way S016: Chil 2A **22**
Haflinger P015: White...................5F **45**
Haig Rd. S050: B'stke 6F **17**
Haileybury Gdns. S030: Hed E.......2A **34**
Halden Cl. S051: Rom...................3E **7**
Hales Dr. S030: Hed E 6G **33**
Halifax Cl. S030: W End................1C **32**
Hallett Cl. S018: South.................1A **32**
Hall Lands La. S050: Fair O 1G **17**
Halstead Rd. S018: South 1H **31**
HALTERWORTH 5F **7**
Halterworth Cl. S051: Rom............5E **7**
Haltons Cl. S040: Tott 2C **26**
Halyard Cl. S031: Lwr Swan.......... 5B **44**
Halyards S031: Hamb 3G **47**
Hamble Way S040: Tott................6E **27**
HAMBLE CLIFF 4C **46**
Hamblecliff Ho. S031: Hamb.........4C **46**
Hamble Cliff Stables
S031: Hamb...............................4C **46**
Hamble Cl. S031: Wars 6A **48**
Hamble Ct. S053: Cha F 2F **15**
Hamble Ct. Bus. Pk.
S031: Hamb...............................4E **47**
Hamble Ho. Gdns. S031: Hamb..... 5G **47**
Hamble La. S031: Burs 6F **43**
Hamble La. S031: Hamb 6F **43**
Hamble La. S031: Hou 6F **43**

Hill Pl. – Jo Jo's Health & Fitness

Hill Pl. SO31: Burs 5H **43**
Hillside Av. SO18: South 2G **31**
Hillside Cl. SO53: Cha F 1F **15**
Hillside M. SO31: Sar G 1B **48**
Hillsons Rd. SO30: Curd 4F **35**
Hill St. SO19: South 2F **41**
Hill St. SO40: Calm 4B **18**
HILLSTREET 4B **18**
Hilltop Dr. SO19: South 1D **42**
Hillview Rd. SO45: Hythe 3C **52**
Hillyfields SO16: Nur 5B **20**
HILLYFIELDS 6B **20**
HILTINGBURY 4F **9**
Hiltingbury Cl. SO53: Cha F 4F **9**
Hilton Rd. SO30: Hed E 5A **34**
Hinkler Ct. SO19: South 1D **42**
Hinkler Rd. SO19: South 5E **33**
Hinton Cres. SO19: South 6E **33**
Hirst Rd. SO45: Hythe 3F **53**
Hispano Av. PO15: White 6G **45**
Hobart Dr. SO45: Hythe 3E **53**
Hobb La. SO30: Hed E 6B **34**
Hobson Way SO45: Holb 5C **54**
Hocombe Rd. SO53: Cha F 3C **8**
Hocombe Wood Rd.
SO53: Cha F 3C **8**
Hodder Cl. SO53: Cha F 2D **14**
Hoddinott Rd. SO50: E'leigh 5H **15**
Hodinott Cl. SO51: Rom 2E **7**
Hoe La. SO51: Toot 5A **12**
Hoe La. SO52: N Bad 4C **12**
Hogarth Cl. SO19: South 3C **42**
Hogarth Cl. SO51: Rom 4E **7**
Hoglands Pk. 4F **5** (1C **40**)
Hogwood La. SO30: W End 3D **24**
HOLBURY 4C **54**
Holbury Drove SO45: Holb 5B **54**
Holcroft Ho. SO19: South 5E **33**
Holcroft Rd. SO19: South 6E **33**
Holkham Cl. SO16: South 6C **20**
Holland Cl. SO53: Cha F 4E **15**
Holland Pk. SO31: Loc H 4D **48**
Holland Pl. SO16: South 2F **29**
Holland Rd. SO19: South 3F **41**
Holland Rd. SO40: Tott 4B **26**
Hollingbourne Cl. SO18: South 3F **31**
Hollman Dr. SO51: Rom 5A **6**
Hollowbread Gdns.
SO31: Old N 4F **43**
Hollybank Cl. SO45: Hythe 3E **53**
Hollybank Rd. SO45: Hythe 3C **52**
Hollybrook Av. SO16: South 6G **21**
Hollybrook Cl. SO16: South 1F **29**
Hollybrook Gdns. SO31: Loc H 2E **49**
Hollybrook Rd. SO16: South 1G **29**
Holly Cl. SO31: Sar G 4C **48**
Holly Cl. SO45: Hythe 1A **54**
Holly Ct. PO15: White 5H **45**
Holly Dell SO16: Bass 4A **22**
Hollydene Vs. SO45: Hythe 2E **53**
Holly Gdns. SO30: W End 6D **24**
Holly Hatch Rd. SO40: Tott 5E **27**
Holly Hill SO16: Bass 4A **22**
Holly Hill Cl. SO16: Bass 4A **22**
Holly Hill La. SO31: Sar G 3A **48**
Holly Hill Mans. SO31: Sar G 3C **48**
Holly Hill Woodland Pk. 3B **48**
Holly Lodge SO17: South 2D **30**
Holly Lodge SO53: Cha F 4E **15**
Holly M. SO16: Bass 5B **22**
Hollyoak Ct. SO16: South 5E **21**
Holly Oak Rd. SO16: South 6E **21**
(not continuous)
Holly Pl. SO16: South 6H **21**
Holly Rd. SO40: A'hst 3A **36**
Holly Rd. SO45: Blac 5E **55**
Hollywood Bowl Eastleigh 5B **16**
Hollywood Bowl
Southampton 4D **4** (1B **40**)
Hollywood Cl. SO52: N Bad 3C **12**
Holmes Cl. SO31: Net A 1A **46**
Holmesland Dr. SO30: Botl 4D **34**
Holmesland La. SO30: Botl 4D **34**
Holmesland Wlk. SO30: Botl 4D **34**
Holmgrove PO14: Titch C 4G **49**
Holmsley Cl. SO18: South 4C **32**
Holmsley Ct. SO40: Tott 3B **26**
Holt Ct. SO19: South 5G **41**
Holt Rd. SO15: South 4B **30**
Holt Vw. SO50: B'stke 6E **17**
Holyborne Rd. SO51: Rom 5E **7**
Holyrood Av. SO17: South 1D **30**
Holy Rood Est.
SO14: South 5F **5** (2C **40**)
(off Orchard La.)
Holyrood Ho.
SO14: South 5E **5** (2C **40**)
Holyrood Pl.
SO14: South 5E **5** (2C **40**)
Homeborough Ho. SO45: Hythe 2E **53**
Home Farm Cl. SO45: Hythe 4F **53**
Homefield SO51: Rom 3C **6**
Home Fld. Dr. SO16: Nur 4A **20**
Homemead Ho. SO51: Rom 5A **6**
Homepoint Ho. SO18: South 4A **32**
Home Rule Rd. SO31: Loc H 3F **49**
Homespinney Ho. SO18: South 1F **31**
Honeysuckle Cl. SO31: Loc H 2E **49**
Honeysuckle Cotts.
SO16: S'ing 5E **23**
Honeysuckle Rd. SO16: Bass 5C **22**
Honeysuckle Rd. SO16: S'ing 5C **22**
Honeysuckle Way SO53: Cha F 1C **14**
Honister Cl. SO16: South 3C **28**
Hood Cl. SO31: Loc H 3F **49**
Hood Rd. SO18: South 3A **32**
HOOK 2E **51**
Hook Cl. SO51: Ampf 3B **8**
Hook Cres. SO51: Ampf 3B **8**
Hook La. PO14: Abs 2E **51**
Hook La. SO31: Wars 2E **51**
HOOK PARK 3A **50**
Hook Pk. Est. SO31: Wars 3A **50**
Hook Pk. Rd. SO31: Wars 2A **50**
Hook Rd. SO51: Ampf 2A **8**
Hookwater Cl. SO53: Cha F 3C **8**
Hookwater Rd. SO53: Cha F 3C **8**
Hook with Warsash Local
Nature Reserve 3A **50**
Hookwood La. SO51: Ampf 3A **8**
Hooper Dr. SO51: Rom 1E **7**
Hope Rd. SO30: W End 1E **33**
Horder Cl. SO16: Bass 6B **22**
Hornbeam Cl. SO30: Hed E 5B **34**
Hornbeam Gdns. SO30: W End 6D **24**
Hornbeam Rd. SO53: Cha F 1A **14**
Hornby Cl. SO31: Wars 1B **50**
Hornchurch Rd. SO16: South 4D **20**
Horne Cl. SO18: W End 1B **32**
Horns Drove SO16: Rown 4B **20**
Horns Hill SO16: Nur 3B **20**
Horns Hill Cl. SO16: Nur 3B **20**
Horsebridge Way SO16: Rown 4C **20**
Horsecroft SO51: Rom 4C **6**
Horsefair, The SO51: Rom 5A **6**
Horsefair Ct. SO51: Rom 5A **6**
Horsefair M. SO51: Rom 5A **6**
Horseshoe Bri. SO17: South 3D **30**
Horseshoe Cl. PO14: Titch C 5H **49**
Horseshoe Dr. SO40: Calm 1A **26**
Horseshoe Dr. SO51: Rom 2E **7**
Horseshoe Lodge SO31: Wars 6C **48**
Horton Way SO50: B'stke 6E **17**
HOUND 1E **47**
Hound Cl. SO31: Net A 2C **46**
Hound Rd. SO31: Hou 2C **46**
Hound Rd. SO31: Net A 2C **46**
Hound Way SO31: Net A 1C **46**
Houndwell Pk. 3E **5** (1C **40**)
Houndwell Pl.
SO14: South 4F **5** (1C **40**)
HOUNSDOWN 6F **27**
Hounsdown Av. SO40: Tott 6F **27**
Hounsdown Bus. Pk.
SO40: Tott 1F **37**
Hounsdown Cl. SO40: Tott 6F **27**
Hoveton Gro. SO53: Cha F 5C **8**
Howard Cl. SO18: S'ing 5G **23**
Howard Cl. SO50: Fair O 2F **17**
Howard Cl. SO53: Cha F 3F **15**
Howard Oliver Ho. SO45: Hythe 3F **53**
Howard Rd. SO15: South 5H **29**
Howard's Gro. SO15: South 3G **29**
Howell Cl. SO14: South 6E **31**
Howerts Cl. SO31: Wars 2B **50**
Hub Eastleigh, The 4C **16**
Hudson Ct. SO40: Tott 5C **26**
Hudson Ho. SO14: South 6G **5** (2D **40**)
(off Royal Cres. Rd.)
Hughes Cl. SO45: Blac 4E **55**
Hulles Way SO52: N Bad 3C **12**
Hulse Lodge SO15: South 3B **30**
Hulse Rd. SO15: South 3B **30**
Hulton Cl. SO19: South 4F **41**
Humber Gdns. SO31: Burs 4G **43**
Hundred, The SO51: Rom 5B **6**
Hungerford SO31: Burs 6F **43**
Hunt Av. SO31: Net A 1B **46**
Hunter Cl. SO45: Hard 2B **54**
Hunter Ct. SO15: South 2F **29**
Hunters Ct. SO31: Burs 1H **43**
Hunters Cres. SO40: Tott 5B **26**
Hunters Cres. SO51: Rom 3F **7**
Hunters Hill SO40: Tott 2C **36**
Hunter's Ride SO21: Hurs 1A **8**
Hunters Way SO50: B'stke 6F **17**
Huntingdon Cl. PO14: Titch C 6G **49**
Huntingdon Cl. SO40: Tott 2E **27**
Huntly Way SO18: South 4H **31**
Hunton Cl. SO16: South 6H **21**
Hunts Cl. SO21: Col C 4G **11**
Hunts Pond Rd. PO14: Titch C 5G **49**
Hunts Pond Rd. SO31: P Ga 2F **49**
Hurdles, The PO14: Titch C 5H **49**
Hurlingham Gdns. SO16: Bass 4C **22**
Hurricane Dr. SO16: Rown 3C **20**
Hursley Dr. SO45: Blac 5E **55**
Hursley Rd. SO21: Hurs 2C **8**
Hursley Rd. SO53: Cha F 3C **8**
Hurstbourne Pl. SO19: South 5H **41**
Hurst Cl. SO40: Tott 3F **27**
Hurst Cl. SO53: Cha F 3C **14**
Hurst Grn. Cl. SO19: South 4A **42**
Hurworth Ho. SO19: South 3F **41**
(off John Thornycroft Rd.)
Hut Farm Pl. SO53: Cha F 2E **15**
Hutwood Rd. SO16: Chil 1C **22**
Huxley Cl. SO31: Loc H 5F **49**
Huxley Ct. SO45: Dib P 4A **52**
Hyde Cl. SO15: South 2G **29**
Hyde Cl. SO40: Tott 4B **26**
Hymans Way SO40: Tott 4F **27**
Hyssop Cl. PO15: White 6H **45**
HYTHE 2E **53**
HYTHE HOSPITAL 4E **53**
Hythe Marine Pk. SO45: Hythe 2F **53**
Hythe Rd. SO40: March 5C **38**
Hythe Sailing Club 3G **53**
Hythe Spartina Marsh
Nature Reserve 3G **53**

I

Ibsen Cl. PO15: White 5G **45**
Ida Ct. SO19: South 3H **41**
Ilex Cres. SO31: Loc H 4D **48**
Imber Way SO19: South 1C **42**
Imperial Av. SO15: South 3F **29**
Imperial Pk. Ind. Est.
SO14: South 4D **30**
Imperial Rd. SO14: South 4D **30**
Imperial Way SO15: South 6G **29**
Ingersley Ri. SO30: W End 2E **33**
Ingle Glen SO45: Dib P 5E **53**
Ingle Grn. SO40: Calm 2B **26**
Ingleside SO31: Net A 6C **42**
Ingleton Rd. SO16: South 2B **28**
Inglewood Gdns. SO50: Fair O 1F **17**
Ingram Ct. SO17: South 3E **31**
Inkerman Rd. SO19: South 2F **41**
Intl. Way SO19: South 5G **41**
Ionic Cl. SO53: Cha F 6H **9**
Ipley Way SO45: Hythe 4E **53**
Irene Ct. SO16: South 1F **29**
Iris Rd. SO16: Bass 5D **22**
Ironbridge Cres. SO31: P Ga 1E **49**
Ironside Ct.
SO14: South 5D **4** (2B **40**)
(off Hamtun St.)
Irving Rd. SO16: South 2D **28**
Irwell Cl. SO53: Cha F 2C **14**
Isis Cl. SO16: South 3C **28**
Islander Wlk. SO50: E'leigh 1H **23**
Isle of Wight Car
Ferry Terminal 6D **4** (3B **40**)
ITCHEN 2F **41**
Itchen Av. SO50: B'stke 6E **17**
Itchen Bri., The 6H **5** (2E **41**)
Itchen Bus. Pk. SO17: South 1E **31**
Itchen College Sports Cen. 6A **32**
Itchen Grange SO50: E'leigh 4D **16**
Itchenside Cl. SO18: S'ing 5H **23**
Itchen Valley Country Pk. 4C **24**
Itchen Valley Country Pk.
Visitor Cen. 4B **24**
Itchen Valley Nature Reserve 5A **24**
Itchen Vw. SO18: S'ing 5H **23**
Ivanhoe Rd. SO15: South 2H **29**
Ivor Cl. SO45: Holb 4C **54**
Ivy Cl. SO40: Tott 1E **27**
Ivy Dene SO19: South 1D **42**
Ivy La. SO18: W End 1B **32**
Ivy La. SO30: W End 1C **32**
Ivy Rd. SO17: South 3E **31**
Ivy Ter. SO30: Hed E 5H **33**

J

Jacaranda Cl. PO15: Seg 3H **49**
Jack Cl. SO53: Cha F 1A **14**
Jackdaw Ri. SO50: E'leigh 6F **15**
Jackie Wigg Gdns. SO40: Tott 4G **27**
Jackman's Cl. SO19: South 2F **41**
Jacksons Rd. SO30: Hed E 2A **34**
Jacobs Cl. SO51: Rom 5C **6**
Jacob's Gutter La. SO40: Elin 6F **27**
(not continuous)
Jacob's Gutter La. SO40: Tott 6F **27**
(not continuous)
Jacob's Wlk. SO40: Tott 1E **37**
James Grieve Av. SO31: Loc H 5E **49**
Jameson Rd. SO19: South 2H **41**
James St. SO14: South 3G **5** (1D **40**)
James Weld Cl. SO15: South 4B **30**
Janaway Gdns. SO17: South 3F **31**
Janes Cl. SO45: Blac 5E **55**
Janson Rd. SO15: South 4G **29**
Jarvis Flds. SO31: Burs 5H **43**
Jasmine Ct. PO15: White 4H **45**
Jasmine Ct. SO17: South 3B **30**
(off Westwood Rd.)
Jasmine Rd. SO30: Hed E 3H **33**
Java Dr. PO15: White 6G **45**
Jazmine Ct. SO31: Net A 1B **46**
Jeffries Cl. SO16: Rown 4C **20**
Jelico Ct. SO16: Bass 4C **22**
Jellicoe Dr. SO31: Sar G 3D **48**
Jellicoe Ho. SO30: Hed E 4B **34**
Jenkyns Cl. SO30: Botl 4E **35**
Jenner Way SO51: Rom 4F **7**
Jennings Rd. SO40: Tott 3G **27**
Jensen Ct. SO15: South 3B **30**
Jermyns La. SO51: Ampf 1F **7**
Jerome Ct. SO19: South 5D **32**
Jerome St. PO15: White 4G **45**
Jerram Pl. SO31: Sar G 3E **49**
Jerrett's La. SO16: Nur 6B **20**
Jersey Cl. SO16: South 6C **20**
Jesmond Gro. SO31: Loc H 6E **49**
Jessamine Rd. SO16: South 1F **29**
Jessica Cres. SO40: Tott 2A **26**
Jessie Ter. SO14: South 6F **5** (2C **40**)
Jetty Rd. SO45: F'ley 1H **55**
Jex Blake Cl. SO16: South 5F **21**
Jockey La. SO50: B'stke 2E **17**
Joe Bigwood Cl. SO16: Nur 4B **20**
John Bunyan Cl. PO15: White 5G **45**
John Darling Mall
SO50: E'leigh 3A **16**
John Hansard Gallery 1D **4** (6B **30**)
Johnson St. SO14: South 3F **5** (1C **40**)
(not continuous)
John's Rd. SO19: South 3F **41**
John St. SO14: South 6F **5** (2C **40**)
John Thornycroft Rd.
SO19: South 3E **41**
Joiners M. SO19: South 3F **41**
Jo Jo's Health & Fitness 3C **30**

A-Z Southampton 67

Leicester Rd. – Manor Quay

Leicester Rd. SO15: South 1H **29**
Leigh Ct. SO50: E'leigh 4G **15**
Leigh Rd. SO17: South 2C **30**
Leigh Rd. SO50: E'leigh 4G **15**
Leigh Rd. SO53: Cha F 3E **15**
Leighton Av. SO15: South 3F **29**
Leighton Rd. SO19: South 2G **41**
Leisure World
Southampton .... **4B 4 (1A 40)**
Le Marechal Av. SO31: Old N 3F **43**
Lemon Rd. SO15: South 4F **29**
Lennox Cl. SO16: South 4D **20**
Lennox Cl. SO53: Cha F 6G **9**
Leonards Ct. SO16: South 3A **28**
Lepe Rd. SO45: Blac 5E **55**
Lepe Rd. SO45: F'ley 5E **55**
Lepe Rd. SO45: Lepe 5E **55**
Leroux Cl. SO15: South 1C **4** (6B **30**)
Leslie Loader Ct. SO50: E'leigh 2A **16**
Leslie Loader Ho. SO19: South 6G **31**
Le Tissier Ct. SO15: South 5A **30**
Leven Cl. SO53: Cha F 6C **8**
Lewes Cl. SO50: E'leigh 1A **16**
Lewin Cl. SO21: Col C 5F **11**
Lewins Wlk. SO31: Burs 4F **43**
Lewis Cl. SO45: Dib P 4A **52**
Lewis Ho. SO14: South 2F **5** (6C **30**)
Lewis Silkin Way SO16: South 5E **21**
Lewry Cl. SO30: Hed E 4A **34**
Lexby Rd. SO40: Elin 5G **27**
Leybourne Av. SO18: South 3H **31**
Leyton Rd. SO14: South 5E **31**
Liberty Row SO31: Hamb 5G **47**
.... *(off Meadow La.)*
Library Rd. SO40: Tott 4G **27**
Lichen Way SO40: March 3D **38**
Lichfield Rd. PO14: Titch C 4G **49**
Liddel Way SO53: Cha F 2D **14**
Lightning Cl. SO45: F'ley 4F **55**
Lilac Rd. SO16: Bass 5D **22**
Lilley Cl. SO40: March 3D **38**
Lime Av. SO19: South 6A **32**
Lime Cl. SO19: South 6A **32**
Lime Cl. SO21: Col C 5G **11**
Lime Cl. SO45: Dib P 5B **52**
Lime Gdns. SO30: W End 6D **24**
Lime Kiln La. SO45: Holb 3B **54**
Lime Kiln La. Est. SO45: Holb 3A **54**
Limes, The SO40: March 4E **39**
Lime St. SO14: South 5F **5** (2C **40**)
Lime Wlk. SO30: Botl 4D **34**
Lime Wlk. SO45: Dib P 5B **52**
Linacre Rd. SO19: South 6D **32**
Lincoln Cl. PO14: Titch C 4G **49**
Lincoln Cl. SO51: Rom 3E **7**
Lincoln Ct. SO15: South 1A **30**
Lincoln Ct. SO30: W End 1C **32**
Lincoln Pl. SO53: Cha F 3F **15**
Lincolns Ri. SO50: E'leigh 5B **10**
Linda Rd. SO45: F'ley 2H **55**
Linden Ct. SO18: W End 6B **24**
Linden Ct. SO31: Loc H 3F **49**
Linden Ct. SO51: Rom 5B **6**
Linden Gdns. SO30: Hed E 6B **34**
Linden Gdns. SO51: Rom 5B **6**
Linden Gro. SO53: Cha F 5E **9**
Linden Rd. SO16: South 5E **21**
Linden Rd. SO51: Rom 5B **6**
Lindoe Cl. SO15: South 4B **30**
Lindsay Rd. SO19: South 5E **33**
Lindway SO31: P Ga 1E **49**
Liners Ind. Est. SO15: South 5G **29**
Linford Ct. SO50: Fair O 2F **17**
Linford Cres. SO16: South 6H **21**
Ling Dale SO16: Chil 2B **22**
Lingdale Pl. SO17: South 3C **30**
Lingfield Gdns. SO18: South 1H **31**
Lingwood Cl. SO16: Bass 2B **22**
Lingwood Wlk. SO16: Bass 2B **22**
Link Rd. SO16: South 6D **20**
Links Vw. Way SO16: Bass 3B **22**
Linnets, The SO40: Tott 3B **26**
Linnet Sq. SO50: E'leigh 6F **15**
Linwood Cl. SO45: Hythe 4E **53**
Lionheart Way SO31: Burs 4F **43**
Lipizzaner Flds. PO15: White 5F **45**
Lisbon Rd. SO15: South 5H **29**
Litchfield Cres. SO18: South 2H **31**
Litchfield Rd. SO18: South 2H **31**
Lit. Abshot Rd. PO14: Abs 1F **51**
Littlefield Cres. SO53: Cha F 1A **14**
Lit. Fox Dr. SO31: P Ga 2F **49**
LITTLE HOLBURY 3B **54**
Lit. Holbury Pk. Homes
SO45: Holb 3A **54**
Lit. Kimble Wlk. SO30: Hed E 5A **34**
Lit. Lance's Hill SO19: South 4H **31**
Lit. Meads SO51: Rom 5A **6**
Lit. Oak Rd. SO16: Bass 5B **22**
Lit. Park Cl. SO30: Hed E 5H **33**
Lit. Park Farm Rd. PO15: Seg 2G **49**
Lit. Quob La. SO30: W End 1E **33**
Littlewood Gdns.
SO30: W End 2D **32**
Littlewood Gdns.
SO31: Loc H 4C **48**
Liverpool St. SO14: South 4C **30**
Livingstone Rd. SO14: South 3C **30**
Lloyd Av. SO40: March 4C **38**
Loane Rd. SO19: South 2H **41**
Lobelia Rd. SO16: S'ing 5E **23**
Lockerley Cres. SO16: South 2D **28**
Locke Rd. SO30: Hed E 3A **34**
LOCKS HEATH 4E **49**
Locks Heath Pk. Rd.
SO31: Loc H 6F **49**
Locksley Ct. SO15: South 4B **30**
Locksley Rd. SO50: E'leigh 6G **15**
Locks Rd. SO31: Loc H 5E **49**
Lockswood Keep SO31: Loc H 3E **49**
Lockswood Rd. SO31: Loc H 6C **48**
Lockswood Rd. SO31: Sar G 6C **48**
Lockswood Rd. SO31: Wars 6C **48**
Lodge, The SO15: South 4B **30**
Lodge Rd. SO14: South 4C **30**
Lodge Rd. SO31: Loc H 4F **49**
Lofting Cl. SO50: B'stke 5E **17**
Logan Cl. SO16: South 4D **20**
Lomax Cl. SO30: Hed E 2A **34**
London Rd.
SO15: South 1D **4** (5B **30**)
Lone Eagle Cl. SO19: South 6D **32**
Longacres PO14: Titch C 3G **49**
Longbridge Cl. SO40: Calm 1C **26**
Longbridge Ct. SO40: Calm 1C **26**
Longbridge Ind. Pk.
SO14: South 6H **5** (2E **41**)
Longclose Rd. SO30: Hed E 4B **34**
LONG COMMON 2D **34**
LONG DOWN 5G **37**
Long Dr. SO30: W End 1E **33**
Longfield Rd. SO50: Fair O 2G **17**
Long La. SO31: Burs 5G **43**
Long La. SO40: March 4B **38**
Long La. SO45: Hard 2B **54**
Long La. SO45: Holb 2B **54**
Longleat Gdns. SO16: South 5F **21**
Longmead Av. SO50: B'stke 3D **16**
Longmeadow Gdns.
SO45: Hythe 2E **53**
Longmead Rd. SO18: South 1A **32**
Longmore Av. SO19: South 3F **41**
Longmore Cres. SO19: South 3F **41**
Longridge Rd. SO30: Hed E 6A **34**
Longstock Cl. SO19: South 5A **42**
Lonsdale Gdns. SO31: Burs 3G **43**
Loperwood La. SO40: Calm 5A **18**
.... (not continuous)
Lord Mountbatten Cl.
SO18: S'ing 5G **23**
Lordsdale Ct. SO16: South 1G **29**
LORD'S HILL 5D **20**
Lords Hill Centre E.
SO16: South 5D **20**
Lords Hill Centre W.
SO16: South 5D **20**
Lords Hill Way SO16: South 5C **20**
Lordswood SO50: Highb 6E **11**
Lordswood Cl. SO16: South 5H **21**
Lordswood Ct. SO16: South 5G **21**
Lordswood Gdns. SO16: South ... 5H **21**
Lordswood La. SO16: Chil 1H **21**
Lordswood Rd. SO16: South 5G **21**
Loreille Gdns. SO16: Rown 2C **20**
Lorne Pl. SO18: South 4A **32**
Loroux Wlk. SO40: Tott 3F **27**
Lortemore Pl. SO51: Rom 5A **6**
Loughwood Cl. SO50: E'leigh 1A **16**
Louis Rd. PO14: Titch C 1H **51**
Lovage Gdns. SO40: Tott 4B **26**
Lovage Rd. PO15: White 6H **45**
Love La. SO51: Rom 5B **6**
Loveridge Way SO50: E'leigh 4A **16**
Lwr. Alfred St. SO14: South 5D **30**
Lwr. Banister St. SO15: South 5B **30**
Lwr. Brownhill Rd.
SO16: South 1A **28**
Lwr. Canal Wlk.
SO14: South 6E **5** (3C **40**)
Lwr. Church Rd. PO14: Titch C 4G **49**
Lwr. Duncan Rd. SO31: P Ga 2F **49**
Lwr. Moors Rd. SO21: Col C 4F **11**
Lwr. Mortimer Rd. SO19: South ... 2F **41**
Lwr. Mullins La. SO45: Hythe 4C **52**
Lwr. New Rd. SO30: W End 1D **32**
Lwr. Northam Rd. SO30: Hed E 5A **34**
Lower St Helens Rd.
SO30: Hed E 6A **34**
Lwr. Spinney SO31: Wars 2A **50**
LOWER SWANWICK 5B **44**
Lwr. Swanwick Rd.
SO31: Lwr Swan 5B **44**
Lower Test Nature Reserve **2G 27**
Lwr. Vicarage Rd. SO19: South 2F **41**
Lwr. William St. SO14: South 5F **31**
Lwr. William St. Ind. Est.
SO14: South 5F **31**
Lwr. York St. SO14: South 5F **31**
LOWFORD 3F **43**
Lowford Hill SO31: Burs 4F **43**
Lowford Hill Cl. SO31: Burs 4G **43**
Lowry Gdns. SO19: South 3C **42**
Lucas Cl. SO16: Rown 4D **20**
Luccombe Pl. SO15: South 1H **29**
Luccombe Rd. SO15: South 1H **29**
Lucerne Gdns. SO30: Hed E 4G **33**
Lucia Foster Welch Halls
SO14: South 6G **5** (2D **40**)
.... *(off Royal Cres. Rd.)*
Ludlow Rd. SO19: South 1G **41**
Lukes Cl. SO31: Hamb 5G **47**
Lukin Dr. SO16: Nur 3A **20**
Lulworth Bus. Cen. SO40: Tott 1E **27**
Lulworth Cl. SO16: South 1C **28**
Lulworth Cl. SO53: Cha F 4D **14**
Lulworth Grn. SO16: South 1C **28**
Lumpy La. SO14: South 1H **5** (6D **30**)
Lumsden Av. SO15: South 4G **29**
Lumsden Mans. SO15: South 4G **29**
Lundy Cl. SO16: South 4C **20**
Lunedale Rd. SO45: Dib P 5B **52**
Lupin Rd. SO16: S'ing 4E **23**
Luton Rd. SO19: South 1B **42**
Lutyens Cl. SO19: South 2D **42**
Luxton Cl. SO30: Botl 4D **34**
Lyburn Cl. SO16: South 5G **21**
Lyburn Ct. SO16: South 5G **21**
Lydgate Cl. SO19: South 1D **42**
Lydgate Grn. SO19: South 1D **42**
Lydgate Rd. SO19: South 1D **42**
Lydiard Cl. SO50: E'leigh 2A **16**
Lydlynch Rd. SO40: Tott 4E **27**
Lydney Rd. SO31: Loc H 4D **48**
Lyme Cl. SO50: E'leigh 2H **15**
Lymer La. SO16: Nur 3A **20**
Lymer Vs. SO16: Nur 3A **20**
Lyndale Rd. SO31: P Ga 3F **49**
Lynden Ga. SO19: South 2A **42**
Lyndhurst Rd. SO40: A'hst 5A **36**
Lyndock Cl. SO19: South 3G **41**
Lyndock Pl. SO19: South 3G **41**
Lynn Cl. SO18: W End 6B **24**
Lynn Cres. PO14: Titch C 6H **49**
Lynton Ct. SO40: Tott 5E **27**
Lynton Rd. SO30: Hed E 4A **34**
Lynx Cl. SO50: B'stke 6E **17**
Lyons Pl. SO30: Hed E 6H **33**
Lyon St. SO14: South 5C **30**
Lytham Rd. SO18: South 2A **32**
Lytton Rd. SO45: Hythe 4F **53**

M

M3 Trade Pk. SO50: E'leigh 3G **15**
Macarthur Cres. SO18: South 3A **32**
McGovern M. SO31: Wars 1A **50**
Mackenzie Cl. SO31: Wars 6B **48**
Macnaghten Rd. SO18: South 4F **31**
Maddison St.
SO14: South 4D **4** (1B **40**)
Maddoxford La. SO32: Botl 2D **34**
Maddoxford Way SO32: Botl 2D **34**
Maffey Ct. SO30: Botl 4E **35**
Magazine La. SO40: March 3D **38**
Magdalene Way PO14: Titch C 5G **49**
Magellan Ho.
SO14: South 6G **5** (2D **40**)
.... *(off Royal Cres. Rd.)*
Magistrates' Court
Southampton **5C 30**
Magnolia Cl. SO45: Dib 3A **52**
Magnolia Gro. SO50: Fair O 1H **17**
Magnolia Rd. SO19: South 6H **31**
Magpie Dr. SO40: Tott 4C **26**
Magpie Gdns. SO19: South 1C **42**
Magpie La. SO50: E'leigh 5G **15**
Maidman Pl. SO30: Hed E 1H **43**
Main Rd. SO21: Col C 2F **11**
Main Rd. SO21: Ott 3B **10**
Main Rd. SO40: March 4D **38**
Main Rd. SO40: Tott 1E **37**
Main Rd. SO45: Dib 5E **39**
Main Rd. SO45: Hard 2B **54**
Mainstream Ct. SO50: B'stke 4D **16**
Majestic Rd. SO16: Nur 6H **19**
Malcolm Cl. SO31: Loc H 4F **49**
Malcolm Cl. SO53: Cha F 5G **9**
Malcolm Rd. SO53: Cha F 4G **9**
Malcroft M. SO40: March 4E **39**
Maldon Cl. SO50: B'stke 4D **16**
Maldon Rd. SO19: South 6G **31**
Malibres Rd. SO53: Cha F 5H **9**
Malin Cl. SO16: South 5C **20**
Mall, The SO53: Cha F 6G **9**
Mallard Cl. SO51: Rom 5C **6**
Mallard Gdns. SO30: Hed E 1A **34**
Mallards, The SO40: Tott 3G **27**
Mallards Rd. SO31: Burs 6F **43**
Mallett Cl. SO30: Hed E 2C **34**
Mallow Cl. SO31: Loc H 5D **48**
Mallow Rd. SO30: Hed E 5G **33**
Malmesbury Cl. SO50: Fair O 1F **17**
Malmesbury Ct. SO31: Net A 2A **46**
Malmesbury Pl. SO15: South 4H **29**
Malmesbury Rd. SO15: South 4H **29**
Malmesbury Rd. SO51: Rom 4B **6**
Malory Cl. SO19: South 5D **32**
Malthouse, The SO51: Rom 5B **6**
Malthouse Cl. SO51: Rom 5A **6**
Malthouse Gdns. SO40: March ... 4D **38**
Malvern Cl. SO50: Fair O 4G **17**
Malvern Dr. SO45: Dib P 4B **52**
Malvern Gdns. SO30: Hed E 1B **34**
Malvern Rd. SO16: South 1G **29**
Malwood Av. SO16: South 6H **21**
Malwood Gdns. SO40: Tott 3C **26**
Malwood Rd. W. SO45: Hythe 3C **52**
Manaton Way SO30: Hed E 2H **33**
Manchester Rd. SO31: Net A 2A **46**
Mandela Way
SO15: South 1A **4** (6A **30**)
Manley Rd. SO31: Burs 4F **43**
Manners, The SO31: Net A 1B **46**
Manns Cl. SO18: W End 1C **32**
Manor Cl. SO31: Old N 4F **43**
Manor Cl. SO40: Tott 5E **27**
Manor Ct. PO15: Seg 3H **49**
Manor Cres. SO31: Burs 4F **43**
Manor Farm Botley **1D 44**
Mnr. Farm Cl. SO50: B'stke 5E **17**
Manor Farm Country Pk. **2B 44**
Mnr. Farm Grn. SO21: Twy 1F **11**
Mnr. Farm Gro. SO50: B'stke 5E **17**
Mnr. Farm Rd. SO18: South 2F **31**
Manor Ho. Av. SO15: South 5C **28**
Manor Pk. Ind. Est.
SO40: Tott 4H **27**
Manor Quay SO18: South 4F **31**

A-Z Southampton 69

Manor Rd. – Mitchell Point

Manor Rd. SO16: Chil 1H **21**
Manor Rd. SO45: Holb 4B **54**
Manor Rd. SO50: B'stke 5E **17**
Manor Rd. Nth. SO19: South 1G **41**
Manor Rd. Sth. SO19: South........ 2G **41**
Manor Ter. SO31: Old N 4E **43**
Mnr. Way SO50: E'leigh 3G **15**
Mnr. Wharf SO18: South 4E **31**
Mansbridge Cotts. SO18: S'ing... 5H **23**
Mansbridge Rd. SO18: S'ing....... 5G **23**
Mansbridge Rd. SO50: E'leigh 6A **16**
Mansel Ct. SO16: South.................1C **28**
Mansell Cl. SO45: Dib P 5B **52**
Mansel Rd. E. SO16: South..........2C **28**
Mansel Rd. W. SO16: South...........1B **28**
Mansergh Wlk. SO40: Tott...........3A **26**
Mansfield Pk. St. SO18: South.....4C **32**
Mansion Ho. Cl. SO31: Sar G........ 2D **48**
Mansion Rd. SO15: South 5G **29**
Manston Ct. SO16: South............ 5D **20**
Maple Cl. SO31: Burs 5F **43**
Maple Cl. SO51: Rom 6F **7**
Maple Gdns. SO40: Tott 5C **26**
Maple Ri. PO15: White.................. 5H **45**
Maple Rd. SO18: South 4G **31**
Maples, The SO53: Cha F...............6E **9**
Maple Sq. SO50: E'leigh................ 6G **15**
Mapleton Rd. SO30: Hed E............5B **34**
Maplewood Cl. SO40: Tott............5B **26**
Maplin Rd. SO16: South 1B **28**
Marathon Pl. SO50: B'stke 5G **17**
MARCHWOOD.................................4D **38**
Marchwood By-Pass
SO40: Tott.......................................5F **27**
Marchwood Ind. Pk.
SO40: March.....................................2E **39**
Marchwood Rd. SO15: South.......5F **29**
Marchwood Rd. SO40: Elin 1H **37**
Marchwood Ter. SO40: March..... 3D **38**
.... *(off Main Rd.)*
Marchwood Yacht Club **2E 39**
Marcus Cl. SO50: B'stke................ 6G **17**
Marcus Liebherr Pavilion **4B 38**
Mardale Rd. SO16: South 3B **28**
Mardale Wlk. SO16: South 3B **28**
Mardon Cl. SO18: S'ing................ 4G **23**
Margam Av. SO19: South 6H **31**
Marianne Cl. SO15: South 5D **28**
Marie Rd. SO19: South..................2C **42**
Marina Dr. SO31: Hamb................ 5G **47**
Marine Pde.
SO14: South......................4H **5** (1D **40**)
Mariners Cl. SO31: Hamb............ 3G **47**
Mariners M. SO45: Hythe 2E **53**
Mariners Way SO31: Wars 6A **48**
Marion Ho. SO31: P Ga...................1F **49**
Maritime Av. SO40: March 2E **39**
Maritime Chambers
SO14: South.......................6G **5** (3D **40**)
....*(off Canute Rd.)*
Maritime Wlk. SO14: South......... 3D **40**
Maritime Way SO14: South 3C **40**
Marjoram Way PO15: White 6H **45**
Mark Cl. SO15: South 4F **29**
Marken Cl. SO31: Loc H 4D **48**
Market Bldgs. SO16: S'ing............5F **23**
Mkt. Pl. SO51: Rom 5A **6**
Mkt. St. SO50: E'leigh...................6B **16**
.... (not continuous)
Marlborough Ct. SO45: Dib P.......4C **52**
Marlborough Ct. SO53: Cha F......3C **14**
Marlborough Gdns.
SO30: Hed E..................................... 6H **25**
Marlborough Ho. SO15: South 3B **30**
Marlborough Rd. SO15: South 3F **29**
Marlborough Rd. SO53: Cha F...... 4G **9**
Marlhill Cl. SO18: South 1H **31**
Marlowe Ct. SO19: South 4H **41**
Marls Rd. SO30: Botl 4C **34**
Marne Rd. SO18: South..................4A **32**
Marsh, The SO45: Hythe................2E **53**
Marshall Ct. SO15: South 4B **30**
Marshall Dr. SO30: W End.............2F **33**
Marshall Sq. SO15: South 4B **30**
Marshfield Cl. SO40: March 4B **38**
Marsh Gdns. SO30: Hed E.............1A **34**
Marsh Ho. SO14: South..... 5F **5** (2C **40**)
Marsh La. SO14: South......5G **5** (2D **40**)
Marsh La. SO45: F'ley 2H **55**
Marsh Pde. SO45: Hythe 2E **53**
.... *(off The Marsh)*
Marston Rd. SO19: South 6D **32**
Martindale Ter. SO16: South 3C **28**
.... *(off Severn Rd.)*
Martins, The SO50: Fair O 2G **17**
Martley Gdns. SO30: Hed E..........1A **34**
Marvin Cl. SO30: Botl 5C **34**
Marvin Way SO18: South...............5C **32**
Marvin Way SO30: Botl 4C **34**
Maryat Way PO15: White............. 4G **45**
Marybridge Cl. SO40: Tott.............5E **27**
Mary Drake Cl. SO45: Holb 5C **54**
Maryfield SO14: South 4G **5** (1D **40**)
Mary Key Cl. SO19: South..............5A **42**
Maryland Cl. SO18: South 6H **23**
Masefield Cl. SO50: E'leigh 4H **15**
Masefield Grn. SO19: South 5D **32**
Matheson Rd. SO16: South 3D **20**
Matley Gdns. SO40: Tott 4B **26**
Matrix Pk. PO15: Titch 4H **49**
Maud Av. PO14: Titch C 6H **49**
Maunsell Way SO30: Hed E........... 6H **25**
Mauretania Ho. SO14: South.........5E **31**
Mauretania Rd. SO16: Nur 5H **19**
Maxwell Rd. SO19: South..............2A **42**
Maybray King Way
SO18: South.................................... 4H **31**
MAYBUSH.......................................1C **28**
Maybush Ct. SO16: South..............2E **29**
Maybush Rd. SO16: South 1C **28**
May Cres. SO45: Holb....................5C **54**
Maycroft Ct. SO15: South..............3B **30**
Mayfair Ct. SO30: Botl 4E **35**
Mayfair Gdns. SO15: South 4B **30**
Mayfield Av. SO40: Tott.................3E **27**
Mayfield Rd. SO17: South 6D **22**
Mayflower Cl. SO53: Cha F 2D **14**
Mayflower Ct. SO16: South...........3F **29**
Mayflower Cruise Terminal 1G **39**
Mayflower Gym, The.........1C 4 (6B 30)
Mayflower Memorial 6D 4 (2B 40)
....*(off Town Quay)*
Mayflower Pk....................6C 4 (2B 40)
Mayflower Rd. SO15: South..........3F **29**
Mayflowers, The SO16: Bass 5C **22**
Mayflower Theatre 1C 4 (6B 30)
Maynard Rd. SO40: Tott................4F **27**
Maypole Vs. SO50: E'leigh............5B **10**
Mayridge PO14: Titch C............... 4G **49**
May Rd. SO15: South.................... 4G **29**
Maytree Cl. SO31: Loc H 4E **49**
Maytree Cl. SO50: Fair O 1G **17**
Maytree Rd. SO18: South..............5A **32**
Maytree Rd. SO53: Cha F 3E **9**
Mayvale Cl. SO40: March 4D **38**
Meacher Cl. SO40: Tott 3E **27**
Mead, The SO45: Hythe.................4C **52**
Meadbrook Gdns.
SO53: Cha F.......................................1E **15**
Mead Cl. SO51: Rom 5E **7**
Mead Ct. SO53: Cha F 1E **15**
..........................*(off Meadbrook Gdns.)*
Mead Cres. SO18: S'ing...................6F **23**
Meadcroft Cl. SO31: Wars...........1A **50**
Meadow Av. SO31: Loc H 3E **49**
Meadow Cl. SO30: W End...............1E **33**
Meadow Cl. SO40: Tott....................6F **27**
Meadow Cl. SO52: N Bad 4E **13**
Meadowcroft Cl. SO21: Ott 2C **10**
Meadow Gro. SO53: Cha F 3E **15**
Meadowhead Rd. SO16: Bass......6B **22**
Meadow La. SO31: Hamb.............. 5G **47**
Meadow La. SO50: E'leigh 5A **16**
Meadowmead Av.SO15: South.....4E **29**
Meadows, The SO18: S'ing 5G **23**
Meadows, The SO51: Rom..............3C **6**
Meadowside Cl. SO18: S'ing........ 5G **23**
Meadowside Leisure Cen.
Whiteley 5H 45
Mdw. Way SO45: F'ley.................. 2G **55**
Mead Rd. SO53: Cha F 1E **15**
Meads, The SO51: Rom 5A **6**
Meads, The SO53: Cha F................2C **14**
Mears Rd. SO50: Fair O 2G **17**
Medieval Merchant's
House.................................6D 4 (2B 40)
.... *(off French St.)*
Medina Chambers SO14: South...3B **40**
Medina Cl. SO53: Cha F 2G **15**
Medina Rd. SO15: South 2F **29**
Medlar Cl. SO30: Hed E.................5B **34**
Medley Pl. SO15: South..................4E **29**
Medwall Grn. SO19: South 6D **32**
Medway Dr. SO53: Cha F.................5B **8**
Megan Rd. SO30: W End 1D **32**
Meggeson Av. SO18: South......... 1H **31**
Melbourne Cen., The.......................1D 40
Melbourne Gdns. SO30: Hed E.....6A **34**
Melbourne Rd. SO30: Hed E.........5A **34**
Melbourne St.
SO14: South.......................4H **5** (1D **40**)
Melbury Ct. SO17: South...............2C **30**
Melchet Rd. SO18: South 3C **32**
Melick Cl. SO40: March................. 3D **38**
Melrose Ct. SO40: Calm 2B **26**
Melrose Rd. SO15: South 1H **29**
Melville Cl. SO16: South.............. 4G **21**
Melville Gdns. SO31: Sar G 1D **48**
Mendip Gdns. SO45: Dib P...........4B **52**
Mendip Rd. SO16: South 3D **28**
Menzies Cl. SO16: South 4D **20**
MEON..5H **51**
Meon Cl. SO51: Rom 5F **7**
Meon Ct. SO18: South 3D **32**
Meon Cres. SO53: Cha F 1F **15**
Meon Rd. PO14: Titch................... 5H **51**
Meon Rd. SO51: Rom 5F **7**
Mercator Cl. SO16: South............ 1D **28**
Mercer Way SO51: Rom 4C **6**
Merchants Wlk.
SO14: South......................6D **4** (2B **40**)
Mercury Cl. SO16: South............. 5D **20**
Mercury Gdns. SO31: Hamb........ 3G **47**
Mercury Marshes Local
Nature Reserve.................................3G 47
Merdon Av. SO53: Cha F 6E **9**
Merdon Cl. SO53: Cha F 6F **9**
Mere Cft. PO15: Seg..................... 4H **49**
Meredith Gdns. SO40: Tott...........5C **26**
Meredith Towers SO19: South 1E **43**
Meridians Cross SO14: South..... 3D **40**
Meridian Way SO14: South 5E **31**
Merlin Gdns. SO30: Hed E........... 4H **33**
Merlin Lodge SO19: South 2F **41**
Merlin Quay SO19: South 1E **41**
Mermaid Way SO14: South 3D **40**
Merrick Way SO53: Cha F...............5B **8**
Merridale Rd. SO19: South........... 1G **41**
Merrieleas Cl. SO53: Cha F 6E **9**
Merrieleas Dr. SO53: Cha F............6E **9**
Merriemeade Cl. SO45: Dib P.......5C **52**
Merriemeade Pde. SO45: Dib P....5C **52**
Merritt Ct. SO53: Cha F 4F **15**
Merrivale Cl. SO45: Hythe 3C **52**
Merryfield PO14: Titch C 3G **49**
Merry Gdns. SO52: N Bad 3E **13**
MERRY OAK.....................................6H **31**
Merryoak Grn. SO19: South 6H **31**
Merryoak Rd. SO19: South 1H **41**
Mersea Gdns. SO19: South 1A **42**
Mersham Gdns. SO18: South.......4A **32**
Merton Rd. SO17: South............... 6D **22**
Mescott Mdws. SO30: Hed E....... 1H **33**
Methuen St. SO14: South 4C **30**
Metuchen Way SO30: Hed E 1A **44**
Mews, The SO16: Rown................ 3D **20**
Mews, The SO45: Blac.....................5F **55**
Mews, The SO53: Cha F 4E **15**
Mews Ct. SO21: Ott 3B **10**
Meynell Cl. SO50: E'leigh 4H **15**
Michael's Way SO45: Hythe 2C **52**
Michaels Way SO50: Fair O............ 1G **17**
Michelmersh Cl. SO16: Rown 4C **20**
Michigan Way SO40: Tott...............3A **26**
MIDANBURY 2H **31**
Midanbury B'way.
SO18: South..................................... 2H **31**
Midanbury Ct. SO18: South.......... 3G **31**
Midanbury Cres. SO18: South..... 2H **31**
Midanbury La. SO18: South 4G **31**
Midanbury Wlk. SO18: South...... 3H **31**
Middlebridge St. SO51: Rom..........5A **6**
Middle Copse SO31: Loc H...........2F **49**
Middle Rd. SO19: South 2H **41**
Middle Rd. SO31: P Ga 2F **49**
Middle Rd. SO52: N Bad..................3E **13**
Middle St. SO14: South 4C **30**
Middleton Cl. SO18: South 1A **32**
Middleton M. SO31: P Ga 2F **49**
Midhurst Ct. SO53: Cha F..............2E **15**
Midlands Est. SO30: W End..........1C **32**
Midway SO45: Hythe 4C **52**
Milbury Cres. SO18: South............5A **32**
Miles Pl. SO31: Wars......................6E **49**
Milford Gdns. SO53: Cha F........... 1G **15**
Milkwood Ct. SO40: Tott 4B **26**
Millais Rd. SO19: South................ 2G **41**
MILLBANK 6E **31**
Millbank Ho. SO14: South 5E **31**
Millbank St. SO14: South 6E **31**
Millbank Wharf SO14: South........6E **31**
Millbridge Gdns. SO19: South......1B **42**
MILLBROOK 4E **29**
Millbrook Cl. SO53: Cha F 2D **14**
Millbrook Flyover SO15: South 4C **28**
Millbrook Ho. SO30: Hed E............4C **34**
Millbrook Point Rd.
SO15: South 6D **28**
.... (not continuous)
Millbrook Rd. SO15: South 4C **28**
Millbrook Rd. E.
SO15: South......................1A **4** (5G **29**)
Millbrook Rd. W. SO15: South.......5F **29**
Millbrook Station (Rail) Hants.....5F **29**
Millbrook Towers SO16: South.....1C **28**
Millbrook Trad. Est.
SO15: South 5D **28**
Mill Cl. SO16: Nur 4B **20**
Millcourt SO50: Fair O.................. 2G **17**
Miller's Pond Gdns.
SO19: South..................................... 2H **41**
Millers Vw. SO31: Burs.................. 3G **43**
Mill Est. Yd. SO16: Nur 4A **20**
Mill Gdns. SO18: W End 6B **24**
Mill Hill SO30: Botl 5E **35**
Mill Ho. Bus. Cen. SO19: South 1F **41**
Mill Ho. Cen. SO40: Tott 4G **27**
Milliken Cl. SO45: F'ley 4F **55**
Mill La. SO16: Nur 5E **19**
Mill La. SO51: Rom...........................5A **6**
Mill Pond, The SO45: Holb............2A **54**
Mill Rd. SO15: South 4D **28**
Mill Rd. SO40: Tott 4G **27**
Millstream Ri. SO51: Rom...............5A **6**
Mill St. SO50: E'leigh.....................3B **16**
Mill Way SO40: Tott.......................6E **27**
Milne Cl. SO45: Dib P 4A **52**
Milner Ct. SO15: South 3G **29**
Milne St. PO15: White.................... 4G **45**
Milton Gro. SO31: Loc H................5F **49**
Milton Rd. SO15: South 5A **30**
Milton Rd. SO50: E'leigh................2B **16**
Milverton Cl. SO40: Elin 6G **27**
Milverton Ct. SO18: South............4B **32**
Milverton Rd. SO40: Elin.............. 5G **27**
Mimosa Dr. SO50: Fair O 1H **17**
Minchin Acres SO30: Hed E.........1A **34**
Minchin Rd. SO51: Rom 2E **7**
MINOR INJURIES UNIT (ROYAL
SOUTH HANTS HOSPITAL)...........5D 30
Minstead Av. SO18: South.............3C **32**
Minstead Ct. SO17: South 3C **30**
................................*(off Westwood Rd.)*
Minster Ct. SO15: South............... 5G **29**
Mintern Cl. SO50: B'stke 2D **16**
Mirabella Cl. SO19: South 3F **41**
Mirror Cl. SO31: Wars................... 6D **48**
Misselbrook La. SO52: N Bad 4H **13**
Missenden Acres SO30: Hed E 3A **34**
Mistletoe Gdns. SO31: Sar G........1C **48**
Mistral SO14: South 6H **5** (2D **40**)
Mitchell Cl. PO15: Seg.................. 2H **49**
Mitchell Cl. SO19: South 2F **41**
.... *(off Hazel Rd.)*
Mitchell Dr. SO50: Fair O 1F **17**
Mitchell Ho. SO19: South 3F **41**
......................*(off John Thornycroft Rd.)*
Mitchell Point SO31: Hamb 5E **47**

Mitchell Rd. S050: E'leigh............5B 16
Mitchells Cl. S051: Rom 5B 6
Mitchell Way S018: S'ton A 3H 23
Mitre Copse S050: B'stke 5F 17
Moat Cl. S045: Holb 5B 54
Moat Hill S018: South 6H 23
Mollison Ri. P015: White............1H 49
Monarch Cl. S031: Loc H 5E 49
Monarchs Keep S031: Old N.....5E 43
Monastery Rd. S018: South 4G 31
Mon Cres. S018: South 4C 32
Monks Brook Cl.
  S050: E'leigh.........................6G 15
Monks Brook Ind. Pk.
  S053: Cha F............................6G 15
Monks Path La. S'ing................6G 23
Monks Rd. S031: Net A..............1A 46
Monks Wlk. S045: Dib P 5C 52
Monks Way S018: S'ing..............5G 23
Monks Way S050: E'leigh 6G 15
Monks Wood Cl. S016: Bass......3D 22
Monkton La. S040: Tott 5C 26
Monmouth Cl. S053: Cha F 1D 14
Monnow Gdns. S018: W End 2B 32
Montague Av. S019: South.........2D 42
Montague Cl. S019: South 2D 42
Montague Ct. S045: Dib P..........5B 52
Montague Rd. S050: B'stke 4D 16
Montefiore Dr. S031: Sar G 3D 48
Monterey Dr. S031: Loc H 5E 49
Montfort Rd. S051: Rom 6F 7
Montgomery Rd. S018: South.....4A 32
Montgomery Way S053: Cha F ...4D 14
Montpelier Cl. S031: P Ga..........4G 49
Montrose Cl. S030: Botl 5C 34
Monument Ct.
  S014: South 6E 5 (3C 40)
  ....(off Lwr. Canal Wlk.)
Moon Cl. S040: March.................4C 38
Moonscross Av. S040: Tott 1F 37
Moore Cl. S015: South 3B 30
Moore Cl. S051: Rom 1E 7
Moore Cres. S031: Net A..............6C 42
MOORGREEN 1F 33
MOORGREEN HOSPITAL 1F 33
Moorgreen Pk. S030: W End.......1F 33
Moorgreen Rd. S030: W End.......1F 33
Moorhead Ct.
  S014: South 6H 5 (3E 41)
Moorhill Gdns. S018: South 4E 33
Moorhill Rd. S030: W End 3D 32
Moorland Cl. S031: Loc H 3E 49
Moorland Cl. S045: Dib P...........4A 52
Moorlands Cres. S018: South 3B 32
Moors Cl. S021: Col C 4F 11
Mopley S045: Blac 5F 55
Mopley Cl. S045: Blac 5F 55
Mordaunt Rd. S014: South 5C 29
Morgan Le Fay Dr. S053: Cha F ...6A 8
Morgan Rd. S030: Hed E 6A 34
Morland Rd. S015: South 2G 29
Morley Cl. S019: South 5H 31
Morley Gdns. S053: Cha F 5E 9
Morpeth Av. S040: Tott 3F 27
Morris Cl. S045: Dib.....................3A 52
Morrison Cl. S019: South.............2E 43
Morris Rd. S015: South...... 1B 4 (6A 30)
Morse Ct. S031: Net A 1A 46
Mortimer Cl. S031: Net A 1A 46
Mortimer Cl. S040: Tott 2C 26
Mortimer Rd. S019: South 1G 41
Mortimer Rd. S030: Botl 5E 35
Mortimers Dr. S050: Fair O 2G 17
Mortimers La. S050: Fair O 1G 17
Mosaic Cl. S019: South 1F 43
Mosedale Wlk. S016: South........3C 28
Moselle Ct. S015: South 6G 29
Moss Dr. S040: March.................3D 38
Mossleigh Av. S016: Rown 4D 20
Mottisfont Cl. S015: South 5C 29
Mottisfont Lodge S051: Rom......5B 6
Mottisfont Rd. S050: E'leigh 3A 16
Mount, The S016: Bass 5B 22
Mountain Ash Cl. S018: South.....4C 32
Mountbatten Av. S051: Rom........5B 6

Mountbatten Bldg.
  S017: South 5C 22
Mountbatten Bus. Cen.
  S015: South 2A 4 (6H 29)
Mountbatten Dr. S031: Sar G......2D 48
Mountbatten Gallery Romsey......1F 19
Mountbatten Ho.
  S015: South 4D 5 (5B 30)
  ....(off Grosvenor Sq.)
Mountbatten Retail Pk.......2B 4 (1A 40)
Mountbatten Rd. S050: E'leigh 2A 16
Mountbatten Way
  S015: South 2A 4 (6G 29)
Mount Dr. S053: Cha F 3G 15
Mountfield S045: Hythe 2C 52
Mount Ho. Cl. S045: Hythe 1G 53
Mt. Pleasant S051: Rom 5B 6
Mt. Pleasant Ind. Pk.
  S014: South 4D 30
Mt. Pleasant Rd. S014: South 4D 30
Mount Vw. S050: E'leigh 3B 16
Mousehole La. S018: South 3H 31
Mousehole La. S045: Hythe 3E 53
Mowbray Rd. S019: South 1B 42
Muir Ho. S045: Dib P 5C 52
Mulberry Cl. S045: Blac 5E 55
Mulberry Cnr. S053: Cha F 3C 14
Mulberry Ct. S030: W End..........1E 33
Mulberry La. S031: Sar G 2C 48
Mulberry Rd. S040: March...........4D 38
Mulberry Wlk. S015: South 3G 29
Mullen Cl. S019: South 1G 41
Multisports Swimming 1H 23
Munro Cres. S015: South 4D 28
Muria Est. S014: South.................6E 31
Murray Cl. S019: South 5E 33
Mursell Way S031: Hou...............1E 47
Mussett Cl. S040: Tott 4E 27
Mustang Av. P015: White 6F 45
Myrtle Av. S040: Tott...................5C 26
Myrtle Rd. S016: South 5F 21
Myvern Cl. S045: Holb.................5C 54

N

Napier Rd. S019: South 6E 33
Narrow La. S051: Rom.................5A 6
Nash Cl. S045: Dib P 5B 52
Nash Rd. S045: Dib P..................5A 52
Nathaniel Cl. S031: Sar G 3D 48
Navigators Way S030: Hed E......3A 34
Neath Way S053: Cha F 2C 14
Needlespar Ct. S031: Wars.........5D 48
Neilson Cl. S053: Cha F 6E 9
Nelson Cl. S045: Holb 5C 54
Nelson Cl. S051: Rom..................4C 6
Nelson Cl. S045: Hythe 5F 53
Nelson Ga. S015: South 1B 4 (6A 30)
Nelson Hill S015: South...... 2A 4 (6A 30)
Nelson Ind. Pk. S030: Hed E 2H 33
Nelson Rd. S015: South 5G 29
Nelson Rd. S050: B'stke..............3D 16
Nelsons Gdns. S030: Hed E 6H 25
Nelson St. S014: South 5H 5 (1D 40)
Neptune Cr. S016: South.............5D 20
Neptune Ho.
  S014: South 6G 5 (3D 40)
  ....(off Canute Rd.)
Neptune Way
  S014: South 6G 5 (3D 40)
Nerquis Cl. S051: Rom.................5E 7
Netherhill La. S032: Botl..............2F 35
NETLEY ABBEY 2B 46
Netley Castle S031: Net A 1A 46
Netley Cliff S031: Net A 2A 46
Netley Cliff Sailing Club 2A 46
Netley Cl. S053: Cha F 4D 14
Netley Firs Cl. S019: South 1F 43
Netley Firs Rd. S030: Hed E 6G 33
NETLEY HILL 6F 33
Netley Hill Est. S019: South 1F 43
Netley Lodge Cl. S031: Net A......2B 46
NETLEY MARSH 4A 24
Netley Marsh Workshops
  S040: Net M.............................4A 24
Netley Rd. P014: Titch C 6G 49
Netley Sailing Club 4C 46

Nettlestone S031: Net A...............6C 42
Neva Rd. S018: South 3H 31
Neville Dr. S051: Rom 4C 6
Newbridge S031: Net A................1C 46
Newbury Cl. S050: B'stke 6G 17
Newbury Pl. S031: Wars 5D 48
Newbury Rd. S015: South 2G 29
Newcliffe Gdns. S030: Hed E 6H 33
New Cliff Ho. S019: South...........4G 41
Newcombe Rd. S015: South 5A 30
New Cotts. S016: South 1A 28
New Ct. P015: Seg 2H 49
NEW FOREST BIRTH CEN. 4A 36
New Forest Ent. Cen.
  S040: Tott 6E 27
New Forest Wildlife Pk. 5E 37
New Inn Ct. S031: Sar G 1C 48
Newitt Pl. S016: Bass..................3B 22
Newlands Av. S015: South 4G 29
Newlands Cl. S045: Blac 5E 55
Newlands Cl. S053: Cha F 2A 14
Newlands Copse S045: Blac........4F 55
Newlyn Wlk. S051: Rom...............4C 6
Newmans Copse Rd.
  S040: Tott 1G 37
Newman St. S016: South 3F 29
Newport Cl. S053: Cha F..............3C 14
New Rd. S014: South 2E 5 (6C 30)
New Rd. S021: Col C 4F 11
New Rd. S031: Net A 1A 46
New Rd. S031: Swanw.................5D 44
New Rd. S031: Wars 1B 50
New Rd. S040: A'hst....................2B 36
New Rd. S045: Blac 4E 55
New Rd. S045: Hard.....................6G 53
  ....(not continuous)
New Rd. S045: Hythe 2E 53
New Rd. S050: B'stke 6G 17
New Rd. S051: Rom 4C 6
New Ter. S016: Bass 4C 22
Newton La. S051: Rom 5A 6
Newton Rd. S018: South 2G 31
NEWTOWN 1A 50
NEWTOWN 5D 30
NEWTOWN 4B 42
Newtown Ct. S031: Wars 6A 48
Newtown Rd. S019: South 3A 42
Newtown Rd. S031: Wars 2A 50
Newtown Rd. S050: E'leigh 3A 16
Nicholas Rd. S045: Blac..............5E 55
Nichol Rd. S053: Cha F 4F 9
Nicholson Wlk. S016: Rown........3B 20
Nichols Rd. S014: South 1G 5 (6D 30)
NICHOLS TOWN 1F 5 (6C 30)
Nickleby Gdns. S040: Tott 4B 26
Nightingale Av. S050: E'leigh.......6E 15
Nightingale Cl. S031: Burs...........5F 43
Nightingale Cl. S015: South.........5G 29
Nightingale Dr. S040: Tott............3B 26
Nightingale Gro. S015: South 4G 29
Nightingale Ho. S031: Net A........3C 46
Nightingale Ho. S051: Rom..........5C 6
Nightingale M. S031: Loc H 4F 49
Nightingale M. S031: Net A..........3C 46
Nightingale Rd. S015: South 4G 29
Nightingale Wlk. S031: Net A 3B 46
Nile Rd. S017: South 1C 30
Nine Elms M. S050: B'stke...........6E 17
Ninian Cl. S050: Fair O 2F 17
Noads Cl. S045: Dib P 5C 52
Noads Way S045: Dib P 5B 52
Noble Rd. P014: Titch C 1H 51
Noble Rd. S030: Hed E 6B 34
Nob's Crook S021: Col C 5G 11
NOB'S CROOK 5G 11
Nomad Cl. S018: South................2B 32
Nook, The S050: E'leigh 2B 16
Nook Cvn. Pk., The S031: Loc H
  Locks Heath 3F 49
Norbury Gdns. S031: Hamb.........5E 47
Norcliffe Rd. S017: South............3C 30
Norcroft Ct. S016: South 1G 29
Nordik Gdns. S030: Hed E 6A 34
Norfolk Cl. S053: Cha F 4E 15
Norfolk Rd. S015: South 3H 29

Norham Av. S016: South 1G 29
Norham Cl. S016: South...............1G 29
Norlands Dr. S021: Ott.................1C 10
Normandy Cl. S016: Rown...........3C 20
Normandy Ct. S031: Wars...........6A 48
Normandy Way S040: March 2D 38
Norman Gdns. S030: Hed E 6G 33
Norman Ho. S014: South.... 1H 5 (5E 31)
Norman Rd. S015: South..............6H 29
Norman Rd. S045: Blac 5F 55
Norris Cl. S051: Rom....................3F 7
Norris Hill S018: South 2G 31
NORTHAM 5E 31
Northam Bri. 5E 31
Northam Bus. Cen.
  S014: South 5E 31
Northampton La. S045: Blac........5E 55
Northam Rd.
  S014: South 2F 5 (6D 30)
  ....(not continuous)
NORTH BADDESLEY 2E 13
Northbourne Cl. S045: Dib P.......5E 53
Northbrook Ind. Est.
  S015: South 1G 29
Northbrook Rd.
  S014: South 1G 5 (6D 30)
Northcliffe Ho. S016: Nur............3H 19
North Cl. S051: Rom 3F 7
Northcote Rd. S017: South 1E 31
North Cl. S015: South 3F 29
Northdene Rd. S053: Cha F 2E 15
North East Cl. S019: South 6C 32
North East Rd. S019: South 1A 42
Nth. End Cl. S053: Cha F 3E 15
Northern Anchorage
  S019: South 2F 41
Northerwood Cl. S052: N Bad......3C 12
Northfield Rd. S018: South 6H 23
Nth. Front S014: South 2E 5 (6C 30)
  ....(not continuous)
Northlands Gdns.
  S015: South 4A 30
Northlands Rd. S015: South 4A 30
Northlands Rd. S040: Tott 3E 27
Northlands Rd. S045: E'leigh 4A 16
Northlands Rd. S051: Rom 6F 7
Northleigh Cnr. S018: S'ing.........4G 23
Nth. Millers Dale S053: Cha F 4C 8
Northmore Cl. S031: Loc H..........2F 49
Northmore Rd. S031: Loc H 2F 49
Northolt Gdns. S016: South 4E 21
North Rd. S017: South 2E 31
North Rd. S040: March.................3E 39
North Rd. S045: Dib P 4B 52
North Solent Nature Reserve......5H 55
NORTH STONEHAM 2F 23
Nth. Stoneham Pk. Development
  S050: E'leigh...........................1F 23
Northumberland Rd.
  S014:South 1H 5 (6D 30)
  ....(not continuous)
Northwood Cl. S016: Bass 3C 22
Norton Cl. S019: South 2G 41
Norton Welch Cl. S052: N Bad.....4F 13
Norwich Cl. S031: Sar G 3C 48
Norwich Rd. S018: South 1H 31
Noyce Cl. S030: W End 2E 33
Noyce Dr. S050: Fair O 2G 17
NST Campus Southampton..........6C 22
NST City........................1D 4 (6B 30)
Nursery Gdns. S019: South 5B 32
Nursery Gdns. S053: Cha F 4E 15
Nursery Gro. S030: Hed E 6A 34
Nursery Ho. S053: Cha F 1E 15
Nursery Rd. S018: South 2F 31
NURSLING 4B 20
Nursling Ind. Est. S016: Nur.........5H 19
Nursling St. S016: Nur 4A 20
Nutash P014: Titch C...................3G 49
Nutbeem Rd. S050: E'leigh..........5A 16
NUTBURN 2F 13
Nutburn Rd. S052: N Bad............3F 13
Nutfield Cl. S016: South..............6C 20
Nutfield Rd. S016: Rown 3B 20
Nutsea Rd. S016: Nur 5B 20
Nutsey La. S040: Tott..................1E 27
Nutshalling Av. S016: Rown 4B 20

Nutshalling Cl. – Peartree Cl.

Nutshalling Cl. SO40: Calm..........1B **26**
Nutwood Way SO40: Tott............1E **27**

O

O2 Guildhall
Southampton.................**2D 4 (6B 30)**
Oakbank Rd. SO19: South...........2F **41**
Oakbank Rd. SO50: B'stke..........3C **16**
Oak Cl. SO15: South......................3A **28**
Oak Cl. SO45: Dib P......................5B **52**
Oak Coppice Cl. SO50: B'stke......5F **17**
Oak Coppice Rd. PO15: White.....5H **45**
Oakdene SO17: South.................1D **30**
Oakdene SO40: Tott......................4B **26**
Oakdene Ct. SO50: Fair O..............2F **17**
Oak Dr. SO50: Fair O.....................2F **17**
Oakenbrow SO45: Dib P..............4A **52**
Oakfield Gdns. SO16: South.........2F **29**
Oakfield Rd. SO40: Tott................4F **27**
Oakfields SO50: E'leigh.................6A **10**
Oak Grn. Way SO18: South...........3A **32**
Oakgrove Gdns. SO50: B'stke.......5E **17**
Oakgrove Rd. SO50: B'stke..........5E **17**
Oak Hill SO31: Burs......................4H **43**
Oakhill Cl. SO31: Burs...................4H **43**
Oakhill Cl. SO53: Cha F................2G **15**
Oakhill Ct. SO53: Cha F................2G **15**
Oakhill Ter. SO31: Burs.................4H **43**
Oakhurst Cl. SO31: Net A.............1C **46**
Oakhurst Rd. SO17: South...........6C **22**
Oakhurst Way SO31: Net A..........1C **46**
Oakland Dr. SO40: March...............4D **38**
Oaklands, The SO53: Cha F..........4E **15**
Oaklands Av. SO40: Tott................4F **27**
Oaklands Gdns. PO14: Titch C.....6G **49**
Oaklands Mead SO40: Tott..........3F **27**
Oaklands Swimming Pool..........**4D 20**
Oaklands Way PO14: Titch C.......6G **49**
Oaklands Way SO16: Bass...........5B **22**
Oaklands Way SO45: Dib P..........5A **52**
Oak Leaf Cl. SO40: March............5C **38**
Oakleafe Pl. SO53: Cha F.............1E **15**
Oakleigh Cres. SO40: Tott............5E **27**
Oakleigh Sq. SO50: B'stke...........2D **16**
Oakley Cl. SO45: Holb..................4B **54**
Oakley Ct. SO16: South................3F **29**
Oakley Ho. SO15: South................4B **30**
Oakley John Wlk. SO19: South....5H **31**
Oakley Rd. SO16: South................2D **28**
Oakmount Av. SO17: South...........2B **30**
Oakmount Av. SO40: Tott..............3F **27**
Oakmount Av. SO53: Cha F...........3F **15**
Oakmount Mans. SO17: South......2B **30**
Oakridge Rd. SO15: South............3B **28**
Oak Rd. SO19: South....................3F **41**
Oak Rd. SO31: Burs.......................5F **43**
Oak Rd. SO45: Dib P......................5B **52**
Oaks, The SO19: South..................6H **31**
Oaks, The SO31: Burs....................5F **43**
Oak Tree Cl. SO21: Col C..............5F **11**
Oaktree Ct. SO16: Bass..................6A **22**
Oaktree Gdns. SO30: Hed E..........5H **33**
Oaktree Pk. SO30: W End..............5D **24**
Oak Tree Rd. SO18: South..............2F **31**
Oak Tree Way SO50: E'leigh.........2A **16**
Oak Va. SO30: W End.....................6B **24**
Oakville Mans.
SO15: South.....................1C **4** (5B **30**)
.... *(off Devonshire Rd.)*
Oak Wlk. SO50: Fair O....................2F **17**
Oakwood Av. SO21: Ott...................2C **10**
Oakwood Cl. SO21: Ott...................2C **10**
Oakwood Cl. SO31: Wars.................1B **50**
Oakwood Cl. SO51: Rom..................3E **7**
Oakwood Cl. SO53: Cha F................5F **9**
Oakwood Ct. SO30: W End..............6E **25**
Oakwood Ct. SO53: Cha F................5F **9**
Oakwood Dr. SO16: South..............4G **21**
Oakwood Rd. SO53: Cha F..............5F **9**
Oakwood Way SO31: Hamb...........4G **47**
Oatfield Gdns. SO40: Calm...........2C **26**
Oatlands SO51: Rom.......................4C **6**
Oatlands Cl. SO32: Botl.................2D **34**
Oatlands Rd. SO32: Botl................2D **34**
Oatley Wlk. SO45: F'ley.................4F **55**
Obelisk Rd. SO19: South...............3F **41**
Occupation La. PO14: Titch..........1H **51**
Oceana Blvd.
SO14: South......................6E **5** (2C **40**)
Ocean Cruise Terminal..................**3C 40**
Ocean Ga. SO14: South..................3C **40**
Oceanic Way SO40: March.............2F **39**
Ocean Quay SO14: South...............6E **31**
Ocean Rd. SO14: South..................4C **40**
OCEAN VILLAGE................**6G 5 (3D 40)**
Ocean Village Innovation Cen.
SO14: South..................................3D **40**
....................................*(off Ocean Way)*
Ocean Way SO14: South.................3D **40**
Ocknell Gro. SO45: Dib..................3A **52**
O'Connell Rd. SO50: E'leigh.........5G **15**
Octavia Rd. SO18: S'ing..................5G **23**
Odeon Cinema
Southampton...................**4B 4 (1A 40)**
Odiham Cl. SO16: South.................5D **20**
Odiham Cl. SO53: Cha F.................4D **14**
Ogle Rd. SO14: South........3D **4** (1B **40**)
Okement Cl. SO18: W End..............1B **32**
Oldbarn Cl. SO40: Calm..................1C **26**
Old Bitumen Rd. SO45: F'ley.........1H **55**
Old Bri. Cl. SO31: Burs...................4H **43**
Old Bridge Ho. Rd. SO31: Burs.....4H **43**
Oldbury Ct. SO16: South................1B **28**
Old Comn. SO31: Loc H..................3E **49**
Old Common Gdns.
SO31: Loc H...................................3E **49**
Old Cracknore Cl.
SO40: March...................................3D **38**
Old Cricket M. SO15: South............3B **30**
Old Dairy Cl. SO40: Tott..................2E **27**
Oldenburg PO15: White..................5F **45**
Old Farm Dr. SO18: South...............6H **23**
Old Garden Cl. SO31: Loc H...........5G **49**
Old Ivy La. SO18: W End..................1B **32**
Old Magazine Cl. SO40: March.......3D **38**
Old Mill Way SO16: South...............2E **29**
OLD NETLEY..**4E 43**
Old Parsonage Ct. SO21: Ott..........2C **10**
Old Priory Cl. SO31: Hamb.............5G **47**
Old Rectory Ct. SO40: Elin..............6H **27**
Old Redbridge Rd. SO15: South....3A **28**
Old Rd. SO14: South..........6G **5** (3D **40**)
Old Rd. SO51: Rom...........................4C **6**
Old School Cl. SO19: South............1A **42**
Old School Cl. SO31: Net A............6C **42**
Old School Cl. SO45: Hard..............2B **54**
Old School Gdns. SO30: W End.....1E **33**
Old Shamblehurst La.
SO30: Hed E.....................................1A **34**
OLD SHIRLEY.....................................**2E 29**
Old Swanwick La.
SO31: Lwr Swan..............................5B **44**
Old Ter. SO16: Bass..........................4C **22**
Old Well Cl., The SO19: South.......2C **42**
Oleander Cl. SO31: Loc H...............2E **49**
Oleander Dr. SO40: Tott...................3A **26**
Olive Rd. SO16: South.......................5E **21**
Oliver Rd. SO18: S'ing.......................6F **23**
Olivers Cl. SO40: Tott.......................4A **26**
Olympic Way SO50: Fair O...............5G **17**
Omdurman Rd. SO17: South............1C **30**
Omega Ent. Pk. SO53: Cha F..........1E **15**
Onibury Cl. SO18: South...................2A **32**
Onibury Rd. SO18: South..................2A **32**
Onslow Rd. SO14: South...................5C **30**
Orchard, The SO16: Bass..................4D **22**
Orchard, The SO16: Chil....................6A **14**
Orchard, The SO45: Dib P..................4A **52**
Orchard, The SO50: E'leigh..............5A **16**
Orchard Av. SO50: B'stke..................6E **17**
Orchard Cl. SO21: Col C....................4F **11**
Orchard Cl. SO32: Botl......................2D **34**
Orchard Cl. SO40: Tott.......................6F **27**
Orchard Cl. SO45: F'ley.....................2H **55**
Orchard Cl. SO52: N Bad....................2C **12**
Orchard Ct. SO30: Botl......................5C **34**
Orchard Ho.
SO14: South.......................5E **5** (2C **40**)
Orchard La.
SO14: South.......................5F **5** (2C **40**)
Orchard La. SO51: Rom......................5B **6**
Orchard Pl. SO14: South....6E **5** (2C **40**)
Orchard Rd. SO31: Loc H..................5D **48**
Orchard Rd. SO50: Fair O..................1F **17**
Orchards Way SO17: South..............1C **30**
Orchards Way SO30: W End..............2D **32**
Orchard Way SO45: Dib P.................4C **52**
Ordnance Rd. SO15: South...............5C **30**
Ordnance Way SO40: March............2E **39**
Oregon Cl. SO19: South....................1A **42**
Oriana Way SO16: Nur......................5H **19**
Oriel Dr. PO14: Titch C......................6G **49**
Oriental Ter.
SO14: South.......................6E **5** (2C **40**)
Orion Cl. SO16: South.........................5D **20**
Orion Ind. Cen. SO18: S'ing..............4H **23**
Orion's Point SO14: South..................5C **30**
Orkney Cl. SO16: South.......................5C **20**
Ormond Cl. SO50: Fair O.....................5G **17**
Orpen Rd. SO19: South........................2C **42**
Orwell Cl. SO16: South........................2C **28**
Orwell Cres. PO14: Titch C..................5G **49**
Osborne Cl. SO31: Net A......................2C **46**
Osborne Dr. SO53: Cha F......................2G **15**
Osborne Gdns. SO17: South................2E **31**
Osborne Gdns. SO50: Fair O................2H **17**
Osborne Ho.
SO14: South.......................6G **5** (2D **40**)
....*(off Canute Rd.)*
Osborne Rd. SO31: Wars......................1A **50**
Osborne Rd. SO40: Tott........................4G **27**
Osborne Rd. Nth. SO17: South............2E **31**
Osborne Rd. Sth.
SO17: South...3D **30**
Oslands La. SO31: Lwr Swan................6B **44**
Oslo Towers SO19: South.....................5G **41**
Osprey Cl. SO16: South.........................4F **21**
Osprey Cl. SO40: March.........................4C **38**
Osterley Cl. SO30: Botl..........................5C **34**
Osterley Rd. SO19: South......................6G **31**
Oswald Rd. SO19: South.........................3F **41**
OTTERBOURNE...**3B 10**
Otterbourne Hill SO21: Ott....................4A **10**
Otterbourne Ho. SO21: Ott.....................3B **10**
Otterbourne Ho. Gdns.
SO21: Ott...3B **10**
Otterbourne Pk. Wood
& Nature Reserve.................................**4B 10**
Otterbourne Rd. SO21: Comp.................2C **10**
Otterbourne Rd. SO21: Ott.....................2C **10**
Otterbourne Rd. SO21: Shaw..................2C **10**
Otter Cl. SO50: B'stke.............................6F **17**
Ouse Cl. SO53: Cha F...............................6B **8**
Outer Circ. SO16: South..........................5E **21**
Outlands La. SO30: Curd..........................5H **35**
Overbrook SO45: Hythe............................4C **52**
Overbrook Way SO52: N Bad...................2C **12**
Overcliff Ri. SO16: Bass............................5A **22**
Overdell Ct. SO15: South...........................4A **30**
Oviat Cl. SO40: Tott......................................4B **26**
Ovington Ct. SO18: South............................3D **32**
Ovington Gdns. SO50: E'leigh....................1A **24**
Owen Rd. SO50: E'leigh...............................5H **15**
Oxburgh Cl. SO50: E'leigh...........................2H **15**
Oxford Av. SO14: South.........1F **5** (5C **30**)
Oxford M. SO14: South..........6F **5** (2C **40**)
Oxford Rd. SO14: South...............................4C **30**
Oxford St. SO14: South.........6F **5** (2C **40**)
Oxlease Cl. SO51: Rom....................................3C **6**
Oxlease Mdws. SO51: Rom..............................2C **6**
Oyster Quay SO31: Hamb...............................5G **47**
Ozier Rd. SO18: South......................................1A **32**

P

Pacific Cl. SO14: South..............................3D **40**
Packridge La. SO51: Toot...........................6C **12**
Paddock, The SO40: Calm..........................1C **26**
Paddock, The SO50: E'leigh.......................1B **16**
Paddocks, The SO45: F'ley.........................2H **55**
Padwell Rd. SO14: South............................4C **30**
Paget Ho. SO16: Nur...................................3H **19**
Paget St. SO14: South..........5H **5** (2D **40**)
Paignton Rd. SO16: South..........................2D **28**
Paimpol Pl. SO51: Rom.................................5B **6**
Painswick Cl. SO31: Sar G..........................1D **48**
Paling Bus. Pk. SO30: Hed E.......................1H **43**
Pallet Cl. SO21: Col C.....................................5F **11**
Pallot Cl. SO31: Burs.......................................4F **43**
Palmers Cl. SO50: Fair O.................................2G **17**
Palmerston Ho.
SO14: South.......................5E **5** (2C **40**)
....*(off Canal Wlk.)*
Palmerston Pk....................**2E 5 (6C 30)**
Palmerston Rd.
SO14: South.......................2E **5** (6C **30**)
Palmerston St. SO51: Rom.............................5B **6**
Palm Rd. SO16: South......................................6E **21**
Palomino Dr. PO15: White...............................6F **45**
Pandora Cl. SO31: Loc H..................................4C **48**
Pangbourne Cl. SO19: South............................1A **42**
Pansy Rd. SO16: Bass..5C **22**
Pantheon Rd. SO53: Cha F................................6H **9**
Panwell Rd. SO18: South...................................4A **32**
Pardoe Cl. SO30: Hed E......................................6A **34**
Parham Dr. SO50: E'leigh..................................3H **15**
Park Cl. SO40: March..4B **38**
Park Cl. SO45: Hythe...3F **53**
Park Ct. SO15: South..5G **29**
Park Ct. SO51: Rom..2A **12**
Parker Ho. SO19: South...3E **41**
PARK GATE..**2F 49**
Park Ga. Bus. Cen. SO31: P Ga................................1F **49**
Pk. Glen SO31: P Ga..3G **49**
Parkhill Cl. SO45: Holb...5C **54**
Parkland Pl. SO17: South...3C **30**
....*(off Westwood Rd.)*
Parklands SO18: South...2G **31**
Parklands SO31: Sar G...3E **49**
Parklands SO40: Tott..3G **27**
Park La. SO15: South..........1C **4** (6B **30**)
Park La. SO21: Ott.......................................4B **10**
Park La. SO40: March.................................3A **38**
Park La. SO45: Holb....................................4A **54**
Park La. SO50: E'leigh.................................5B **10**
Park M. SO31: P Ga.......................................2F **49**
Park Rd. SO15: South....................................5G **29**
Park Rd. SO53: Cha F......................................5E **9**
Parkside SO40: Tott..6F **27**
Parkside Av. SO16: South..............................3B **28**
Park St. SO16: South..3F **29**
Park Vw. SO14: South.......2F **5** (6C **30**)
....*(off New Rd.)*
Park Vw. SO30: Botl..................................4E **35**
Park Vw. SO30: Hed E..............................4H **33**
Park Vw. SO50: E'leigh............................4A **16**
....*(off Newtown Rd.)*
Parkville Rd. SO16: S'ing.........................5F **23**
Park Wlk. SO14: South.......2E **5** (6C **30**)
Pk. Way SO50: Fair O.................................1H **17**
Parkway, The SO16: Bass...........................4C **22**
Parkway Ct. SO53: Cha F...........................6F **9**
Parkwood Cl. SO30: Hed E........................4B **34**
Parnell Rd. SO50: E'leigh..........................5H **15**
Parry Rd. SO19: South...............................1D **42**
Parsonage Rd. SO14: South........................5D **30**
Partry Cl. SO53: Cha F...............................5B **8**
Passage La. SO31: Wars...............................5H **47**
Passfield Av. SO50: E'leigh..........................6G **15**
Passfield Cl. SO50: E'leigh...........................5G **15**
Pastures, The PO14: Titch C..........................3G **49**
Pastures, The SO50: E'leigh..........................5A **16**
....*(off Cranbury Rd.)*
Pat Bear Cl. SO15: South..............................3A **28**
Patricia Cl. SO30: W End...............................1D **32**
Patricia Dr. SO30: Hed E................................5B **34**
Paulet Cl. SO18: South....................................2A **32**
Paulet Lacave Av. SO16: Nur..........................3B **20**
Pauletts La. SO40: Calm...................................1B **26**
Paulson Cl. SO53: Cha F......................................5E **9**
Pavilion Ct. SO15: South.....................................4A **30**
Pavilion Gdns. SO45: Blac....................................4E **55**
Pavilion Rd. SO30: Botl...4B **34**
Pavilion Rd. SO30: Hed E.......................................4B **34**
Paxton Cl. SO30: Hed E..6B **34**
Paxton Ct. SO31: Loc H...5E **49**
Paynes La. SO50: Fair O...1F **17**
Paynes Pl. SO30: Hed E...2A **34**
Payne's Rd. SO15: South...5G **29**
....(not continuous)
Peach Rd. SO16: South......................................5E **21**
Peacock Trad. Est.
SO50: E'leigh..3G **15**
Peak Cl. SO16: South.....................................3D **28**
Peartree Av. SO19: South...............................1G **41**
Pear Tree Cl. SO32: Botl..................................2D **34**
Peartree Cl. SO19: South..................................1F **41**

72 A-Z Southampton

Peartree Gdns. S019: South........5A **32**
PEARTREE GREEN 1G **41**
Peartree Rd. S019: South.............1F **41**
Peartree Rd. S045: Dib P...............4C **52**
Pebble Ct. S040: March...................3D **38**
Peckham Cl. P014: Titch C............5G **49**
Peel Cl. S051: Rom..........................3F **7**
Peel St. S014: South.............. 1H **5** (6E **31**)
Peewit Hill S031: Burs....................2G **43**
Peewit Hill Cl. S031: Burs..............2G **43**
Pegasus Cl. S016: South................5D **20**
Pegasus Rd. S031: Hamb...............5F **47**
Pembers Cl. S050: Fair O 1G **17**
Pembers Hill Dr. S050: Hor H........1H **17**
Pembrey Cl. S016: South................4D **20**
Pembroke Cl. S050: E'leigh............2H **15**
Pembroke Cl. S051: Rom.................5B **6**
Pembroke Cl. S017: South...............2C **30**
Pembroke Rd. S019: South..............1B **42**
Penarth Cl. S019: South..................5C **32**
Pendle Cl. S016: South...................3D **28**
Pendleton Gdns. S045: Blac 4E **55**
Pendula Way S050: B'stke...............2E **17**
Penelope Gdns. S031: Burs............4F **43**
Penhale Gdns. P014: Titch C..........6F **49**
Penhale Way S040: Tott...................6E **27**
Penistone Cl. S019: South..............3A **42**
Pennard Way S053: Cha F 3C **14**
Pennine Gdns. S045: Dib P.............4A **52**
Pennine Ho. S016: South................4D **28**
Pennine Rd. S016: South................4C **28**
Pennine Way S053: Cha F..............3F **15**
Pennington Cl. S021: Col C.............5F **11**
Pennycress S031: Loc H..................5C **48**
Penrhyn Cl. S050: E'leigh...............2H **15**
Penshurst Way S050: E'leigh..........1A **16**
Pentagon, The S045: F'ley 3G **55**
Pentire Av. S015: South..................2H **29**
Pentire Way S015: South................1H **29**
Pentland Cl. S045: Dib P................4A **52**
Peppard Cl. S018: South.................4A **32**
Peppercorn Way S030: Hed E........6H **25**
Pepys Av. S019: South....................6D **32**
Percivale Rd. S053: Cha F 3B **14**
Percy Rd. S016: South.....................3E **29**
Peregrine Cl. S040: Tott..................5C **26**
Pern Dr. S030: Botl..........................4E **35**
Perran Rd. S016: South...................2B **28**
Perrywood S045: Holb.....................5C **54**
Perrywood Gdns. S040: Tott...........3B **26**
Pershore Cl. S031: Loc H................5E **49**
Persian Dr. P015: White...................6F **45**
Peterborough Rd.
 S014: South.................................4C **30**
Peters Cl. S031: Loc H....................4C **48**
Peterscroft Av. S040: A'hst.............4A **36**
Peters Rd. S031: Loc H...................4C **48**
Pettinger Gdns. S017: South...........3F **31**
Petty Cl. S051: Rom.........................5C **6**
Petworth Gdns. S016: South...........4F **21**
Petworth Gdns. S050: E'leigh 2A **16**
Pevensey Cl. S016: South...............2B **28**
Peverells Wood Av.
 S053: South..6G **9**
Peverill Rd. S019: South.................1G **41**
Pewsey Pl. S015: South..................1H **29**
Phillimore Rd. S016: S'ing...............5F **23**
Phillips Cl. S016: Rown....................3C **20**
Philpot Dr. S040: March..................4D **38**
Phoenix Cl. S031: Burs...................4G **43**
Phoenix Film Theatre, The.............6C **22**
Phoenix Ho. S030: Hed E................4C **34**
Phoenix Ind. Pk. S050: E'leigh........5C **16**
Pickwick Cl. S040: Tott...................4A **26**
Pilchards Av. S050: Fair O...............5G **17**
Pilgrim Pl. S018: S'ing.....................5G **23**
Pilgrims Cl. S053: Cha F 2B **14**
Pimpernel Cl. S031: Loc H..............5C **48**
Pine Cl. S040: A'hst........................3B **36**
Pine Cl. S045: Dib P.......................4C **52**
Pine Cl. S052: N Bad.......................2C **12**
Pine Cres. S053: Cha F 5E **9**
Pine Dr. S018: South.......................4D **32**
Pine Dr. E. S018: South...................4E **33**
Pinefield Rd. S018: South................1H **31**
Pinegrove Rd. S019: South.............2H **41**

Pinehurst S017: South.....................2C **30**
Pinehurst Rd. S016: Bass...............2B **22**
Pinelands Ct. S016: South...............5G **21**
Pinelands Rd. S016: Chil 1B **22**
Pine Rd. S051: Rom.........................6F **7**
Pines, The S016: South...................6F **21**
Pineview Cl. S031: Burs..................4G **43**
Pine Wlk. S016: Chil.......................2A **22**
Pine Wlk. S031: Sar G.....................2E **49**
Pine Way S016: Bass......................2B **22**
Pinewood S016: Bass......................3B **22**
Pinewood Cl. S051: Rom.................3F **7**
Pinewood Cres. S045: Hythe..........5F **53**
Pinewood Dr. S045: Hythe..............5F **53**
Pinewood Pk. S019: South..............6F **33**
Pinto Cl. P015: White......................6G **45**
Piping Cl. S021: Col C.....................5F **11**
Piping Grn. S021: Col C..................5F **11**
Piping Rd. S021: Col C....................5F **11**
Pirelli St. S014: South.........3C **4** (1B **40**)
Pirelli Way S050: E'leigh................5A **16**
Pirrie Cl. S015: South.....................2H **29**
Pitchpond Rd. S031: Wars..............1A **50**
Pitmore Cl. S050: E'leigh................5B **10**
Pitmore Rd. S050: E'leigh...............5B **10**
Pitt Rd. S015: South........................5G **29**
Places Leisure Eastleigh................4G **15**
Plaitford Wlk. S016: South..............2D **28**
Plantation Dr. S040: March..............4C **38**
Platform Rd.
 S014: South........................6E **5** (3C **40**)
Players Cres. S040: Tott..................6E **27**
Plaza M. S051: Rom.........................5C **6**
Plaza Theatre...................................5C **6**
PLEASANT VIEW..............................2B **42**
Plover Cl. S016: South.....................4F **21**
Ploverfield S031: Burs....................5H **43**
Plover Rd. S040: Tott......................4C **26**
Pluto Rd. S050: E'leigh...................4H **15**
Point Eastleigh, The........................4A **16**
Pointout Cl. S016: Bass..................6A **22**
Pointout Rd. S016: Bass.................6A **22**
Polesden Cl. S053: Cha F...............5C **8**
POLYGON.............................1B **4** (5A **30**)
Polygon, The
 S015: South.........................1B **4** (6A **30**)
Polygon Ct. S015: South 1B **4** (6A **30**)
Polymond Ho.
 S014: South........................6D **4** (2B **40**)
....(off Castle Way)
Pomeroy Cres. S030: Hed E 1H **33**
Pond Cl. S040: March.....................3D **38**
Pondhead Cl. S045: Holb................5C **54**
Pond Rd. S031: Sar G.....................1D **48**
Pond Vw. S018: South.....................1A **32**
Pooksgreen S040: March................3A **38**
POOKSGREEN....................................3A **38**
Poole Rd. S019: South....................1G **41**
Popes Ct. S040: Tott.......................4F **27**
Popes La. S040: Tott.......................4F **27**
Poplar Dr. S040: March..................4B **38**
Poplar Rd. S019: South..................5H **31**
Poplar Way S030: Hed E................5B **34**
Poppy Cl. S031: Loc H....................5D **48**
Poppyfields S053: Cha F................1C **14**
Poppy Rd. S016: S'ing....................4E **23**
Porchester Rd. S019: South...........2G **41**
Porlock Rd. S016: South.................2A **28**
Portal Rd. S019: South...................1B **42**
Portal Rd. S050: B'stke..................4D **16**
Portcullis Ho.
 S014: South........................6F **5** (3C **40**)
Portelet Ho. S016: South................6B **20**
Portelet Pl. S030: Hed E................6A **34**
Porteous Cres. S053: Cha F...........1H **15**
Portersbridge M. S051: Rom...........5B **6**
Portersbridge St. S051: Rom..........5A **6**
Porter's La. S014: South.......6D **4** (2B **40**)
Port Hamble S031: Hamb...............4G **47**
Portland St. S014: South......3D **4** (1B **40**)
Portland Ter.
 S014: South........................2D **4** (1B **40**)
Portside Cl. S040: March................2E **39**
Portsmouth Rd. S019: South..........2F **41**
Portsmouth Rd. S031: Burs............4G **43**
PORTSWOOD.....................................2D **30**

Portswood Av. S017: South............ 3D **30**
Portswood Pk. S017: South............ 3D **30**
PORTSWOOD PARK...........................3D **30**
Portswood Rd. S017: South........... 3D **30**
Portview Rd. S018: South.............. 1H **31**
Portway Cl. S018: South.................4B **32**
Posbrook La. P014: Titch C............4H **51**
Postern Ct.
 S014: South.........................5D **4** (2B **40**)
Postern Ct.
 S014: South.........................3E **5** (1C **40**)
Potters Heron Cl. S051: Ampf.........3A **8**
Potters Heron La. S051: Ampf.......2A **8**
Poulner Cl. S019: South.................4A **42**
Poundbury Ct. S031: Sar G............1E **49**
Pound Ga. Dr. P014: Titch C..........6G **49**
Pound La. S040: Tott......................2E **37**
Pound St. S018: South...................4A **32**
Pound Tree Rd.
 S014: South........................3E **5** (1C **40**)
Powell Cres. S040: Tott..................6F **27**
Precinct, The S030: Hed E.............5A **34**
Precinct, The S045: Holb................4B **54**
Precosa Rd. S030: Botl..................6C **34**
Prelate Way P014: Titch C..............5G **49**
Premier Cen., The S051: Rom........6G **7**
Premier Gym....................................2D **30**
Premier Pde. S018: South...............6H **23**
Premier Way S051: Rom.................2A **12**
Preshaw Cl. S016: South................5G **21**
Prestwood Rd. S030: Hed E...........5A **34**
Pretoria Rd. S030: Hed E...............6H **33**
Priest Cft. S045: Blac.....................4E **55**
Priest Cft. Dr. S045: Blac...............3E **55**
Priestfields P014: Titch C...............5G **49**
Priestlands S051: Rom....................4A **6**
Priestlands Cl. S040: Net M...........5A **26**
Priestley Cl. S040: Tott...................4C **26**
Priestwood Cl. S018: South............4D **32**
Primate Rd. P014: Titch C..............4H **49**
Primrose Cl. S053: Cha F...............3B **14**
Primrose Rd. S016: Bass...............5C **22**
Primrose Way S031: Loc H.............5D **48**
Primrose Way S051: Rom................4F **7**
Prince of Wales Av.
 S015: South.......................................4E **29**
Prince Rd. S016: Rown...................3C **20**
Princes Cl. S014: South..................5E **31**
Princes Ho. S014: South.................5E **31**
....(off Graham St.)
Prince's Rd. S051: Rom...................4B **6**
Princes Rd. S015: South.................5H **29**
PRINCESS ANNE HOSPITAL............6F **21**
Princess Rd. S030: W End..............1E **33**
Princess Rd. S040: A'hst.................3B **36**
Prince's St. S014: South.................5E **31**
Prince William Ct. S050: B'stke.......6E **17**
Prinstead La. S031: Old N...............5E **43**
Priory Av. S017: South....................2F **31**
Priory Cl. S017: South.....................2F **31**
THE PRIORY HOSPITAL
 SOUTHAMPTON...............................5E **39**
Priory Ho. S014: South........ 2F **5** (6C **30**)
Priory Rd. S017: South....................2E **31**
Priory Rd. S031: Net A 1A **46**
Priory Rd. S050: E'leigh..................6H **15**
Proctor Cl. S019: South.................6D **32**
Promenade, The S045: Hythe.........2E **53**
Prospect Pl. S045: Hythe...............1E **53**
Prospect Pl. S053: Cha F...............1E **15**
Prospect Rd. S019: South...............6H **31**
Providence Hill S031: Burs.............3G **43**
Providence Pk. S016: Bass...........4B **22**
Prunus Cl. S016: South..................4G **21**
Pudbrooke Gdns. S030: Hed E........3H **33**
Pudbrook Ho. S030: Botl.................5D **34**
Puffin Cl. S016: South....................4F **21**
Purbrook Cl. S016: South...............5H **21**
Purcell Rd. S019: South..................2D **42**
PureGym Southampton...................1G **29**
PureGym Southampton
 Bitterne..5A **32**
PureGym Southampton
 Central..............................2B **4** (6A **30**)
Purkess Cl. S053: Cha F.................6F **9**
Purlieu Dr. S045: Dib P...................4B **52**
Purvis Gdns. S019: South...............3B **42**
Pycroft Cl. S019: South..................6A **32**

Pyland's La. S031: Burs..................2H **43**
Pylewell Rd. S045: Hythe...............2E **53**

QE2 Activity Cen. 2B **44**
QEII Cruise Terminal.........................5D **40**
Quadrangle, The S050: E'leigh....3A **16**
Quadrangle, The S051: Rom..........6G **7**
Quantock Rd. S016: South.............3C **28**
Quantocks, The S045: Dib P..........4B **52**
Quay, The S031: Hamb...................5G **47**
Quay 2000 S017: South..................3E **31**
Quay Haven S031: Lwr Swan.........6B **44**
Quay La. S031: Lwr Swan...............6B **44**
Quayside S030: Botl........................5E **35**
Quayside S018: South....................4E **31**
Quayside Wlk. S040: March............2D **38**
Quays Swimming & Diving
 Complex, The.....................5C **4** (2B **40**)
Quebec Gdns. S031: Burs..............4F **43**
Queen Elizabeth Ct.
 S017: South.......................................6E **23**
Queens Cl. S045: Hythe..................4F **53**
Queen's Ct. S015: South.....1B **4** (6A **30**)
Queens Ho. S014: South.....5F **5** (2C **40**)
Queens Ride S052: N Bad...............3C **12**
Queen's Rd. S015: South................1G **29**
Queens Rd. S031: Wars.................1A **50**
Queens Rd. S053: Cha F.................4F **9**
Queens Ter.
 S014: South.........................6F **5** (2C **40**)
Queenstown Rd. S015: South..... 5H **29**
Queens Vw. S031: Net A 1A **46**
Queen's Way
 S014: South.........................6E **5** (2C **40**)
Querida Cl. S031: Lwr Swan.........5B **44**
Quilter Cl. S019: South...................1D **42**
Quintilis M. S016: South................5G **21**
Quob Farm Cl. S030: W End..........6E **25**
Quob La. S030: W End...................5E **25**

Rachel Cl. S050: B'stke.................. 5G **17**
Radcliffe Ct.
 S014: South........................1H **5** (5D **30**)
Radcliffe Rd.
 S014: South........................1H **5** (6D **30**)
Radleigh Gdns. S040: Tott............3B **26**
Radley Cl. S030: Hed E..................2A **34**
Radstock Rd. S019: South.............2F **41**
Radway Cres. S015: South............3H **29**
Radway Rd. S015: South................3H **29**
Raeburn Dr. S030: Hed E..............4A **34**
Raglan Cl. S053: Cha F..................3B **14**
Raglan Cl. S031: P Ga....................2F **49**
Raglan Cl. S050: E'leigh................1A **16**
Railway Cotts. S015: South...........3A **28**
Railway Vw. Rd. S017: South.......3E **31**
Rainbow Pl. S015: South................5G **29**
Raleigh Ho. S014: South....4G **5** (1D **40**)
....(off The Compass)
Raley Rd. S031: Loc H...................5E **49**
RAMALLEY...5C **8**
Rampart Rd. S018: South...............4F **31**
Ramsden Rd. S016: South..............1D **28**
Randall Cl. S040: Calm..................1C **26**
Randall Rd. S053: Cha F................3F **9**
Randolph St. S015: South...............4G **29**
....(not continuous)
Ranelagh Ct. S017: South..............3C **30**
....(off Westwood Rd.)
Ranelagh Gdns. S015: South.......4A **30**
Ranfurly Gdns. S045: Dib P...........5C **52**
Range Gdns. S019: South..............2B **42**
Ranger Cl. S014: South.......6H **5** (2B **40**)
Ranmore Cl. S045: Dib....................3A **52**
....(off Rowhill Dr.)
Rapide Cl. S050: E'leigh.................1A **24**
Ratcliffe Rd. S030: Hed E...............4A **34**
Rathdora M. S031: Burs..................5F **43**
RATLAKE...2A **8**
Ratlake La. S021: Hurs....................1A **8**
Rattigan Gdns. P015: White...........5G **45**
Raven Cl. S014: South....................5D **30**
Ravenscroft Cl. S031: Burs............4F **43**

Station Rd. – Tichborne Rd.

Station Rd. SO16: Nur 4G **19**
Station Rd. SO19: South 3H **41**
Station Rd. SO31: Burs 5H **43**
Station Rd. SO31: Net A 2A **46**
Station Rd. SO31: P Ga 2E **49**
Station Rd. SO51: Rom 5B **6**
Station Rd. Nth. SO40: Tott 4H **27**
Station Rd. Sth. SO40: Tott 4H **27**
Steele Cl. SO53: Cha F 3F **15**
Steep Cl. SO18: South 3C **32**
Steeple Way PO14: Titch C 4H **49**
Steinbeck Cl. PO15: White 5G **45**
Stenbury Way SO31: Net A 6C **42**
Stephen Ct. SO45: Holb 5C **54**
Stephens Ct. SO51: Rom 5A **6**
Stephenson Way SO30: Hed E 6H **25**
Steuart Rd. SO18: South 4F **31**
Steventon Rd. SO18: South 4C **32**
Stewart Ho. SO53: Cha F 4E **9**
Stillmeadows SO31: Loc H 5E **49**
Stinchar Dr. SO53: Cha F 2C **14**
Stirling Cl. SO40: Tott 3G **27**
Stirling Cres. SO30: Hed E 2A **34**
Stirling Cres. SO40: Tott 3G **27**
Stirling Wlk. SO51: Rom 5B **6**
Stocklands SO40: Calm 1B **26**
Stockley Cl. SO45: Holb 5B **54**
Stockton Cl. SO30: Hed E 4B **34**
Stoddart Av. SO19: South 5H **31**
STOKE COMMON 2E **17**
Stoke Comn. Rd. SO50: B'stke 2E **17**
Stoke Hgts. SO50: Fair O 5G **17**
STOKE PARK 6E **17**
Stoke Pk. Dr. SO50: B'stke 3D **16**
Stoke Pk. Rd. SO50: B'stke 3D **16**
Stoke Rd. SO16: South 2E **29**
Stokes Ct. SO15: South 5A **30**
.... *(off Archers Rd.)*
Stoke Wood Cl. SO50: Fair O 6G **17**
Stonechat Dr. SO40: Tott 3A **26**
Stonecrop Cl. SO31: Loc H 5D **48**
Stoneham Cemetery Rd.
SO18: S'ing 5H **23**
Stoneham Cl. SO16: S'ing 4F **23**
Stoneham Ct. SO16: Bass 4D **22**
Stoneham Gdns. SO31: Burs 4F **43**
Stoneham Golf Course 3D **22**
Stoneham La. SO16: S'ing 4F **23**
Stoneham La. SO50: E'leigh 6G **15**
Stoneham Way SO16: S'ing 5F **23**
STONEHILLS 3H **55**
Stone Ter. SO21: Ott 4A **10**
Stoney Croft Ri. SO53: Cha F 5E **15**
Stonymoor Cl. SO45: Holb 5B **54**
Stour Cl. SO18: W End 6B **24**
Stourvale Gdns. SO53: Cha F 2F **15**
Stowe Cl. SO30: Hed E 2B **34**
Stragwyne Cl. SO52: N Bad 2C **12**
Straight Mile SO51: Ampf 3G **7**
Stranding St. SO50: E'leigh 4H **15**
Strategic Pk. SO30: Hed E 4F **33**
Stratfield Dr. SO53: Cha F 5C **8**
Stratford Ct. SO16: Bass 4C **22**
Stratford Pl. SO50: E'leigh 3B **16**
Stratton Rd. SO15: South 2G **29**
Strawberry Flds. SO30: Hed E 5G **33**
Strawberry Hill SO31: Loc H 4D **48**
Streamleaze PO14: Titch C 5G **49**
St. End SO52: N Bad 2F **13**
Strides Way SO40: Tott 4B **26**
Strongs Cl. SO51: Rom 4E **7**
Stroudley Way SO30: Hed E 1B **34**
Stuart Bridgewater Ho.
SO18: South 4A **32**
Stubbington Way SO50: Fair O 2G **17**
Stubbs Drove SO30: Hed E 5B **34**
Stubbs Rd. SO19: South 3C **42**
Studland Cl. SO16: South 2B **28**
Studland Rd. SO16: South 3B **28**
Studley Av. SO45: Holb 4B **54**
Sturminster Ho. SO16: South 2E **29**
Suffolk Av. SO15: South 4H **29**
Suffolk Cl. SO53: Cha F 5E **15**
Suffolk Dr. PO15: White 6F **45**
Suffolk Dr. SO53: Cha F 4E **15**
Suffolk Grn. SO53: Cha F 5E **15**
Sullivan Rd. SO19: South 1D **42**
Summerfield Gdns. SO16: S'ing 4F **23**
Summerfields SO31: Loc H 6F **49**
Summerlands Rd. SO50: Fair O 2F **17**
Summers St. SO14: South 5E **31**
Summit Way SO18: South 2H **31**
Sundowner SO14: South 6H **5** (2D **40**)
Sunningdale SO45: Hythe 4C **52**
Sunningdale Cl. SO50: B'stke 5E **17**
Sunningdale Gdns.
SO18: South 4B **32**
Sunningdale Mobile Home Pk.
SO21: Col C 4F **11**
Sunnydale Farm Camping & Cvn. Site
SO31: Old N 5C **42**
Sunnyfield Ri. SO31: Burs 4G **43**
Sunnyside SO31: Loc H 4G **49**
Sunny Way SO40: Tott 4F **27**
Sunset Av. SO40: Tott 3E **27**
Sunset Rd. SO40: Tott 3E **27**
Sunvale Cl. SO19: South 2B **42**
Surbiton Rd. SO50: E'leigh 2B **16**
Surrey Ct. SO15: South 5G **29**
Surrey Ct. SO53: Cha F 4F **15**
Surrey Point SO16: Bass 6A **22**
Surrey Rd. SO19: South 3F **41**
Surrey Rd. SO53: Cha F 4E **15**
SUSSEX PLACE 3D **4** (1C **40**)
Sussex Rd. SO14: South 3E **5** (1C **40**)
Sussex Rd. SO53: Cha F 4F **15**
Sutherland Cl. SO51: Rom 3E **7**
Sutherland Rd. SO16: South 4D **20**
Sutherlands Ct. SO53: Cha F 1E **15**
Suttones Pl. SO15: South 4B **30**
Sutton Rd. SO40: Tott 2E **27**
Swale Dr. SO53: Cha F 6B **8**
Swallow Cl. SO40: Tott 5B **26**
Swallow Sq. SO50: E'leigh 5F **15**
Swanage Cl. SO19: South 1G **41**
Swan Cl. SO31: Lwr Swan 6B **44**
Swanley Cl. SO50: E'leigh 2A **16**
Swanmore Av. SO19: South 2B **42**
Swan Quay SO18: South 3F **31**
Swanton Gdns. SO53: Cha F 6C **8**
SWANWICK 6F **45**
Swanwick Bus. Cen.
SO31: Lwr Swan 6B **44**
SWANWICK HILL 1G **49**
Swanwick Lakes
Nature Reserve 4D **44**
Swanwick La. SO31: Lwr Swan 5A **44**
Swanwick La. SO31: Swanw 5A **44**
Swanwick Shore
SO31: Lwr Swan 6A **44**
Swanwick Shore Rd.
SO31: Lwr Swan 6B **44**
Swanwick Station (Rail) 1F **49**
SWAYTHLING 5F **23**
Swaythling Rd. SO18: W End 6B **24**
Swaythling Rd. SO30: W End 6B **24**
Swaythling Station (Rail) 5F **23**
Sweethills Cres. PO15: White 5F **45**
Swift Cl. SO50: E'leigh 5F **15**
Swift Gdns. SO19: South 4F **41**
Swift Hollow SO19: South 4F **41**
Swift Rd. SO19: South 4F **41**
.... (not continuous)
Swincombe Ri. SO18: W End 2B **32**
Swithuns Ct. SO16: Nur 3H **19**
Sycamore Av. SO53: Cha F 4E **9**
Sycamore Cl. PO14: Titch C 6G **49**
Sycamore Cl. SO31: Burs 5F **43**
Sycamore Cl. SO51: Rom 6F **7**
Sycamore Ct. SO16: South 1F **29**
Sycamore Dr. SO45: Holb 3B **54**
Sycamore Rd. SO16: South 1E **29**
Sycamore Rd. SO45: Hythe 3C **52**
Sycamores, The SO45: Hythe 3E **53**
Sycamore Wlk. SO30: Botl 4E **35**
Sydmanton Rd. SO51: Rom 5C **6**
Sydney Av. SO31: Hamb 4E **47**
Sydney Rd. SO15: South 2F **29**
Sydney Rd. SO50: B'stke 3D **16**
Sylvan Av. SO19: South 5C **32**
Sylvan Ct. SO31: Sar G 3E **49**
Sylvan Dr. SO52: N Bad 3C **12**
Sylvan La. SO31: Hamb 5G **47**
Sylvans, The SO45: Dib P 4A **52**
Sylvia Cres. SO40: Tott 2E **27**
Symes Rd. SO51: Rom 5E **7**
Symonds Cl. SO53: Cha F 3F **15**
Symphony Cl. SO31: Loc H 4C **48**

T

Tadburn Cl. SO53: Cha F 2F **15**
Tadburn Grn. SO51: Rom 5B **6**
Tadburn Meadows Local
Nature Reserve 5E **7**
Tadburn Rd. SO51: Rom 5C **6**
Tadfield Cres. SO51: Rom 5C **6**
Tadfield Rd. SO51: Rom 5C **6**
Talbot Cl. SO16: Bass 5B **22**
Talbot Ct. SO14: South 6E **5** (2C **40**)
Talbot Rd. SO45: Dib P 5B **52**
Talisman Bus. Cen. SO31: P Ga 1F **49**
Talland Rd. PO14: Titch C 6F **49**
Tamar Gdns. SO18: W End 1B **32**
Tamar Gro. SO45: Hythe 3C **52**
Tamarisk Gdns. SO18: South 3G **31**
Tamarisk Rd. SO30: Hed E 4H **33**
Tamella Rd. SO30: Botl 5C **34**
Tamorisk Dr. SO40: Tott 5C **26**
Tanglewood SO40: March 4E **39**
Tangmere Dr. SO16: South 5D **20**
Tangmere Ri. SO53: Cha F 3F **15**
Tanhouse Cl. SO30: Hed E 6B **34**
Tanhouse La. SO30: Botl 6B **34**
.... (not continuous)
Tanhouse La. SO30: Hed E 6B **34**
.... (not continuous)
Tankerville Rd. SO19: South 2F **41**
Tanners, The PO14: Titch C 1G **51**
Tanner's Brook Way
SO15: South 5D **28**
Tanner's Cl. SO16: South 5F **21**
Tanners Rd. SO52: N Bad 4E **13**
Tansy Mdw. SO53: Cha F 3B **14**
Tanyards, The SO53: Cha F 5C **8**
Taplin Dr. SO30: Hed E 3A **34**
Taranto Rd. SO16: South 5G **21**
Tarver Cl. SO51: Rom 2E **7**
Tasman Cl. SO14: South 3D **40**
Tasman Ct. SO14: South 3D **40**
Tatchbury Mount Hill Fort 2A **26**
TATCHBURY MOUNT HOSPITAL 1A **26**
Tate Cl. SO51: Rom 2E **7**
Tate Ct. SO15: South 3A **28**
Tate M. SO15: South 3A **28**
Tate Rd. SO15: South 3A **28**
Tates Rd. SO45: Hythe 4F **53**
.... (not continuous)
Tatwin Cl. SO19: South 6D **32**
Tatwin Cres. SO19: South 6D **32**
Taunton Dr. SO18: South 4B **32**
Tavells Cl. SO40: March 4C **38**
Tavells La. SO40: March 4B **38**
Taverner Cl. SO19: South 2D **42**
Tavistock Cl. SO51: Rom 3E **7**
Tavistock Rd. SO16: South 1D **28**
Tavy Cl. SO53: Cha F 1D **14**
Taylor Cl. SO19: South 4F **41**
Teachers Way SO45: Holb 4B **54**
Teal Cl. SO40: Tott 4C **26**
TeamSport Indoor
Karting Eastleigh 4B **16**
Tebourba Way SO16: South 4C **28**
Tebourba Way SO30: Curd 5H **35**
Ted Bates Ct. SO15: South 5A **30**
Ted Bates Rd.
SO14: South 5H **5** (2D **40**)
Tedder Rd. SO18: South 3A **32**
Tees Cl. SO53: Cha F 6B **8**
Tees Farm Rd. SO21: Col C 5F **11**
Tees Grn. SO21: Col C 5F **11**
Telegraph Rd. SO30: W End 3E **33**
Telegraphy Hgts. SO30: W End 2E **33**
Telford Gdns. SO30: Hed E 1B **34**
Telford Way PO15: Seg 2G **49**
Teme Cres. SO16: South 2C **28**
Teme Rd. SO16: South 3C **28**
Templars Mede SO53: Cha F 4D **14**
Templars Way SO53: Cha F 3B **14**
Temple Gdns. SO19: South 3H **41**
Temple Rd. SO19: South 3H **41**
Tenby Cl. SO18: South 3A **32**
Tenby Dr. SO53: Cha F 3C **14**
Tench Way SO51: Rom 4B **6**
Tennyson Cl. SO45: Holb 3B **54**
Tennyson Ct. SO17: South 2C **30**
Tennyson Rd. SO17: South 3D **30**
Tennyson Rd. SO40: Tott 1C **26**
Tennyson Rd. SO50: E'leigh 6H **15**
Tenpin Southampton 4D **28**
Tenterton Av. SO19: South 4B **42**
Terminus Ter.
SO14: South 6F **5** (2D **40**)
.... (not continuous)
Tern Cl. SO45: Hythe 4F **53**
Terrace, The SO21: Ott 2B **10**
Terrier Cl. SO30: Hed E 6H **25**
Terriote Cl. SO53: Cha F 6E **9**
Testlands Av. SO16: Nur 3B **20**
Test Mill SO51: Rom 5A **6**
Test Rd. SO14: South 4C **40**
Test Valley Bus. Cen.
SO16: South 1H **27**
Test Valley Bus. Pk.
SO52: N Bad 2E **13**
TESTWOOD 2E **27**
Testwood Av. SO40: Tott 2E **27**
Testwood Cres. SO40: Tott 1C **26**
Testwood La. SO40: Tott 3F **27**
Testwood Pl. SO40: Tott 3G **27**
Testwood Rd. SO15: South 5F **29**
Tetney Cl. SO16: South 6C **20**
Teviot Ho. SO14: South 5E **31**
.... *(off York Cl.)*
Teviot Rd. SO53: Cha F 2C **14**
Thackeray Rd. SO17: South 3D **30**
Thacking Grn. SO21: Col C 5F **11**
Thames Cl. SO18: W End 6B **24**
Theo Ho. SO31: P Ga 2F **49**
Thetford Gdns. SO53: Cha F 6B **8**
Thicket, The SO51: Rom 6F **7**
Third Av. SO15: South 4C **28**
Thirlmere SO50: E'leigh 5H **15**
Thirlmere Rd. SO16: South 1C **28**
Thirlstane Firs SO53: Cha F 3D **14**
Thistle Rd. SO30: Hed E 5H **33**
Thistle Rd. SO53: Cha F 2B **14**
Thomas Lewis Way
SO14: South 3D **30**
Thomas Lewis Way
SO16: S'ing 6F **23**
Thomas Lewis Way
SO17: South 2E **31**
Thomas Rd. SO52: N Bad 3E **13**
Thornbury Av. SO15: South 4A **30**
Thornbury Av. SO45: Blac 5E **55**
Thornbury Hgts. SO53: Cha F 4H **9**
Thornbury Wood SO53: Cha F 4H **9**
Thorn Cl. SO50: E'leigh 2A **16**
Thorndike Cl. SO16: South 1E **29**
Thorndike Rd. SO16: South 1D **28**
Thorners Ct. SO15: South 5B **30**
Thorner's Homes SO15: South 3F **29**
Thorness Cl. SO16: South 2B **28**
THORNHILL 6D **32**
Thornhill Av. SO19: South 5D **32**
Thornhill Cl. SO45: F'ley 4F **55**
Thornhill Homes SO19: South 6D **32**
.... *(off Tatwin Cl.)*
THORNHILL PARK 4D **32**
Thornhill Pk. Rd. SO18: South 4D **32**
Thornhill Rd. SO16: South 5H **21**
Thornhill Rd. SO45: F'ley 3F **55**
Thornleigh Rd. SO19: South 3G **41**
Thornton Av. SO31: Wars 6A **48**
Thornycroft Av. SO19: South 3F **41**
Thorold Ct. SO18: South 2G **31**
Thorold Rd. SO18: South 3G **31**
Thorold Rd. SO53: Cha F 5G **9**
Threefield La.
SO14: South 5F **5** (2C **40**)
Three Oaks SO19: South 6E **33**
Thruxton Ct. SO19: South 6G **31**
Thurmell Cl. SO30: Hed E 1A **44**
Thurmell Wlk. SO30: Hed E 1A **44**
Thurston Cl. SO53: Cha F 6F **9**
Thyme Av. PO15: White 5H **45**
Tichborne Rd. SO18: South 3D **32**

A-Z Southampton 77

Tichborne Rd. – Warburton Cl.

Tichborne Rd. SO50: E'leigh........ 1H 23
Tickleford Dr. SO19: South...........5A 42
Tickner Cl. SO30: Botl 6C 34
Ticonderoga Gdns.
SO19: South.............................. 4G 41
Tides Reach SO18: South.............3F 31
Tides Way SO40: March 3D 38
Tilbrook Rd. SO15: South 3E 29
Tillingbourn PO14: Titch C 4G 49
Timberley Cl. SO45: Holb 4B 54
Timor Cl. PO15: White 5F 45
Timsbury Dr. SO16: South........... 2D 28
Timson Cl. SO40: Tott...................5C 26
Tindale Rd. SO16: South..............1C 28
Tinker All. SO18: S'ton A..............2A 24
Tinning Way SO50: E'leigh 4G 15
Tintagel Cl. SO16: South 3G 21
Tintern Gro. SO15: South... 1A 4 (6A 30)
Tiptree Cl. SO50: E'leigh...............2A 16
Titanic Engineers
Memorial........................**1D 4 (6C 30)**
Titchbourne Ho. SO30: Hed E.......5A 34
TITCHFIELD COMMON..................6G 49
TITCHFIELD PARK........................4H 49
Titchfield Pk. Rd. PO15: Seg 4H 49
Tithe Mead SO51: Rom...................3C 6
Tivoli Cl. SO53: Cha F.................... 6H 9
Tolefrey Gdns. SO53: Cha F...........1B 14
Tollbar Way SO30: Hed E............. 2G 33
Tollgate SO53: Cha F.....................5E 15
Tollgate Rd. SO31: Lwr Swan 5B 44
Tomkyns Cl. SO53: Cha F 1B 14
Tommy Grn. Wlk.
SO50: E'leigh.............................. 4H 15
Toogoods Way SO16: Nur.............4B 20
Toomer Cl. SO45: F'ley 3F 55
TOOTHILL......................................6B 12
Toothill Rd. SO51: Toot.................6A 12
Topiary Gdns. SO31: Loc H...........3F 49
Torch Cl. SO50: B'stke................. 5G 17
Torcross Cl. SO19: South.............. 3G 41
Tormead SO45: Hythe...................4C 52
Tornay Gro. SO52: N Bad..............3C 12
Toronto Ct. SO16: South 3D 28
Torquay Av. SO15: South.............. 3H 29
Torque Cl. SO19: South..................1E 43
Torre Cl. SO50: E'leigh..................1A 16
Torridge Gdns. SO18: W End 6B 24
Torrington Cl. SO19: South...........1A 42
Torwood Gdns. SO50: B'stke.........5E 17
Tosson Cl. SO16: South 3C 28
Totland Cl. SO16: South.................3C 28
Totnes Cl. SO50: E'leigh 2H 15
Tottehale Cl. SO52: N Bad 4C 12
TOTTON..4F 27
Totton & Eling Bowls Cen............**4A 26**
Totton & Eling Heritage Cen. **5H 27**
Totton & Eling Tennis Cen. **4B 26**
Totton By-Pass SO40: Tott 5F 27
Totton Health & Leisure Cen. **3C 26**
Totton Station (Rail)......................4G 27
Totton Western By-Pass
SO51: Ower..................................4A 18
Tower Ct. SO31: Wars....................6A 48
Tower Gdns. SO16: Bass 5B 22
Tower Ho. SO19: South.................. 3G 41
Tower La. SO50: E'leigh.................5C 16
Tower La. Ind. Est.
SO50: E'leigh...............................6C 16
Tower Pl. SO30: W End.................. 2D 32
Towers, The SO31: Net A...............2A 46
Townhill Farm District Cen.
SO18: W End................................1B 32
TOWNHILL PARK.............................1B 32
Townhill Way SO18: W End 6B 24
Town Quay SO14: South....6D 4 (2B 40)
Town Wall
Southampton ....**5D 4 (2B 40)**
.... *(off Western Esplanade)*
Toynbee Cl. SO50: E'leigh..............4A 16
Toynbee Rd. SO50: E'leigh 4A 16
Trafalgar Cl. SO53: Cha F............ 2D 14
Trafalgar Rd. SO15: South........... 5G 29
Trafalgar Way SO45: Hythe 5F 53
Tranby Rd. SO19: South 1G 41
Treagore Rd. SO40: Calm 2C 26
Trearnan Cl. SO16: South 3D 28
Treeside Av. SO40: Tott 4G 27
Treeside Rd. SO15: South............. 3G 29
Treloyhan Cl. SO53: Cha F............3F 15
Tremona Ct. SO16: South 1F 29
Tremona Rd. SO16: South 6F 21
Trenley Cl. SO45: Holb...................5B 54
Trent Cl. SO18: South 2H 31
Trent Ho. SO14: South 6E 31
Trent Rd. SO18: South 2H 31
Trent Way SO30: W End................ 1D 32
Tresillian Gdns. SO18: W End........1B 32
Trevone Cl. SO40: Tott...................6E 27
Trevose Cl. SO53: Cha F 3F 15
Trevose Cres. SO53: Cha F............2F 15
Trevose Way PO14: Titch C 6F 49
Triangle, The SO18: South.............2F 31
Triangle Gdns. SO16: Nur..............6B 20
Triangle La. PO14: Titch 5H 51
Trident Bus. Pk. SO45: Hythe 3F 53
Trimaran Rd. SO31: Wars...............6C 48
Trinity Ct. SO15: South 5G 29
Trinity Ct. SO21: Col C 5H 11
Trinity Ct. SO40: March 3D 38
Trinity Ct. SO40: Tott.....................1E 27
Trinity Ct. SO53: Cha F 1F 15
Trinity Ind. Est. SO15: South 4D 28
Trinity Rd. SO14: South 1F 5 (6C 30)
Tripps End Cvn. Site
SO30: Hed E................................5B 34
Tristram Cl. SO53: Cha F 3B 14
Triton Cen., The SO51: Rom 2A 12
TROTTS...2H 37
Trotts La. SO40: March..................1A 38
Trowbridge Cl. SO16: Rown 4C 20
Truro Ri. SO50: B'stke 4E 17
Tudor Cl. SO40: Calm 3B 26
Tudor Gdns. SO30: Hed E 6G 33
Tudor House & Gdns..........**5D 4 (2B 40)**
Tudor Wood Cl. SO16: Bass...........5B 22
Tuffin Cl. SO16: Nur.........................4A 20
Tulip Gdns. SO31: Loc H.................4D 48
Tulip Rd. SO16: Bass 5E 23
Tumulus Cl. SO19: South.................1E 43
Tunstall Cl. SO19: South..................1E 43
Tunstall Rd. SO19: South..................1E 43
Turner Sims Concert Hall **6C 22**
Turners Oak Ct. SO15: South......... 2G 29
Turnpike Way SO30: Hed E 3H 33
Turnstone Gdns. SO16: South 4F 21
Tuscan Wlk. SO53: Cha F............... 1G 15
Tussocks, The SO40: March.......... 3D 38
Tutor Cl. SO31: Hamb 4F 47
Tweed Cl. SO53: Cha F 6C 8
Twiggs End Cl. SO31: Loc H........... 3D 48
Twin Oaks SO30: Botl 4E 35
Twyford Av. SO15: South................ 2G 29
Twyford Ho. SO15: South 4B 30
Twyford Rd. SO50: E'leigh..............4B 16
Twynham Way SO50: B'stke 3D 16
Tyleshades, The SO51: Rom............5C 6
Tyne Cl. SO53: Cha F........................2C 14
Tyne Way SO30: W End 1E 33
Tyrrel Rd. SO53: Cha F 6E 9
Tytherley Rd. SO18: South 3C 32

U

Ullswater SO50: E'leigh..................6A 16
Ullswater Av. SO18: W End 2B 32
Ullswater Rd. SO16: South.............2C 28
Undercliff Gdns. SO16: Bass..........5A 22
Underwood Cl. SO16: Bass 5A 22
Underwood Rd. SO16: Bass 5A 22
Underwood Rd. SO50: B'stke 3D 16
Union Pl. SO15: South 5H 29
Union Rd. SO14: South 5E 31
Unity Ct. SO50: E'leigh.....................5B 16
Universal Marina SO31: Sar G 1A 48
University Cres. SO17: South 6D 22
University of Southampton
Avenue Campus..........................**1C 30**
University of Southampton
Highfield Campus........................**6C 22**
University of Southampton Maritime
Centre of Excellence **5B 22**
University of Southampton National
Oceanography Cen. **4D 40**
University of Southampton
Sports Ground............................**2H 23**
University Parkway SO16: Chil ... 6G 13
University Rd. SO17: South 5D 22
Unwin Cl. SO19: South 4F 41
Uplands Way SO17: South.............1C 30
Upmill Cl. SO30: W End 6B 24
Up. Banister St. SO15: South.........5B 30
Up. Barn Copse SO50: Fair O....... 4G 17
Up. Brook Dr. SO31: Loc H............5C 48
Up. Brownhill Rd. SO16: South.... 6D 20
Up. Bugle St.
SO14: South.......................5D 4 (2B 40)
Up. Deacon Rd. SO19: South 5B 32
Upper Mkt. St. SO50: E'leigh 4B 16
Up. Mead Cl. SO50: Fair O 2G 17
Up. Moors Rd. SO50: B'dge 5F 11
Up. Mullins La. SO45: Hythe.........4C 52
Up. New Rd. SO30: W End 2D 32
Up. Northam Cl. SO30: Hed E...... 5G 33
Up. Northam Dr. SO30: Hed E.......5E 33
Up. Northam Rd. SO30: Hed E..... 4G 33
Up. St Helens Rd. SO30: Hed E.... 1H 43
Up. Shaftesbury Av.
SO17: South 1D 30
UPPER SHIRLEY..............................1H 29
Up. Shirley Av. SO15: South 2G 29
Up. Spinney SO31: Wars...............1A 50
Up. Toothill Rd. SO16: Rown.........6B 12
Up. Weston La. SO19: South.........3A 42
UPTON 3A 20
Upton Cres. SO16: Nur 2B 20
Upton Ho. SO16: South 2D 28
Upton La. SO16: Nur...................... 4G 19
Uxbridge Cl. SO31: Sar G 1D 48

V

Vale, The SO31: Loc H 5F 49
Vale, The SO45: Hythe 4C 52
Vale Dr. SO18: South 2H 31
Valentine Av. SO19: South.............2C 42
Valentine Ct. SO19: South 2C 42
Valerian Rd. SO30: Hed E..............5A 34
Valley Cl. SO21: Col C......................5F 11
Valley Cl. SO45: Blac 4F 55
Valley Ri. SO31: Sar G 3C 48
Valley Rd. SO40: Tott.......................6F 27
Valley Rd. SO53: Cha F.....................6E 9
Vanburgh Ho. SO30: Hed E.............3B 34
Vanburgh Way SO53: Cha F 4C 8
Vanguard Rd. SO18: South..............3A 32
Vardy Cl. SO19: South 2D 42
Varna Rd. SO15: South 6G 29
Vaudrey Cl. SO15: South 2G 29
Vaughan Cl. SO19: South 6E 33
Vaughan Rd. SO45: Dib 3A 52
Veals La. SO40: March 5E 39
Vear's La. SO21: Col C..................... 5G 11
Vectis Ct. SO16: Bass.......................5B 22
Vellan Ct. SO16: South 2B 28
Velmore Rd. SO53: Cha F 3D 14
Velsheda Ct. SO45: Hythe...............1E 53
Ventnor Ct. SO16: Bass 4E 23
Verbena Way SO30: Hed E 5B 34
Verdon Av. SO31: Hamb 4E 47
Verger Cl. PO14: Titch C................. 4G 49
Vermont Cl. SO16: Bass 5B 22
Verne Cl. PO15: White......................4F 45
Vernon Wlk. SO15: South 5B 30
.... *(off Winchester St.)*
Verulam Rd. SO14: South............. 4D 30
Vespasian Ct. SO18: South..............4E 31
Vespasian Quay SO18: South..........3E 31
Vespasian Rd. SO18: South.............4F 31
Vespasian Way SO53: Cha F 1G 15
Vesta Way SO53: Cha F.................. 6G 9
Vicarage Dr. SO30: Hed E............ 6H 33
Vicarage La. SO32: Curd 4G 35
Vicarage Rd. SO40: March 4D 38
Viceroy Rd. SO19: South 2A 42
Victena Rd. SO50: Fair O 1F 17
Victor Ct. SO18: South................... 5D 32
Victoria Cl. SO31: Loc H 6E 49
Victoria Glade SO31: Net A 2C 46
Victoria Lodge SO17: South 2D 30
Victoria M. SO31: Net A..................2A 46
Victoria Pl. SO51: Rom.....................5B 6
.... *(off Love La.)*
Victoria Rd. SO19: South................4F 41
Victoria Rd. SO31: Net A 1A 46
Victoria Rd. SO50: E'leigh 2B 16
Victoria St. SO14: South.... 2H 5 (6E 31)
Victoria Wlk. SO30: W End 1E 33
Victor St. SO15: South 2F 29
Victory Cl. SO53: Cha F 2D 14
Victory Cres. SO15: South 4F 29
Victory Rd. SO15: South..................5F 29
Victory Sq. SO15: South..................5F 29
Victory Way SO16: Rown................2C 20
Viking Cl. SO16: South 5C 20
Viking Cl. SO45: Blac.......................5F 55
Village M. SO40: March.................. 4D 38
Villeneuve St. SO50: E'leigh 4G 15
Villiers Rd. SO15: South 4G 29
Villiers Rd. SO45: Dib P 5C 52
Vincent Av. SO16: South................. 1G 29
Vincent Rd. SO15: South 3G 29
Vincent's Gro. SO15: South 3F 29
Vincent St. SO15: South 3G 29
Vincent's Wlk.
SO14: South 4E 5 (1C 40)
Vine Bank SO18: South 3C 32
Vine Cl. SO31: Sar G 4B 48
Vine Rd. SO16: South 6E 21
Vinery Gdns. SO16: South 1G 29
Vinery Rd. SO16: South 1G 29
Vineyard Cl. SO19: South 2F 41
Vineyards, The SO52: N Bad 3E 13
Viney Av. SO51: Rom........................4E 7
Violet Cl. SO53: Cha F 1C 14
Violet Rd. SO16: Bass......................5C 22
Viscount Gdns. SO50: E'leigh....... 1H 23
Vixen Cl. SO40: A'hst........................1C 36
Vokes Cl. SO19: South.....................6B 32
Vokes Memorial Gdns., The.........**3C 40**
Vosper Rd. SO19: South 3F 41
VT Ho. SO30: Hed E 3B 34
Vue Cinema Eastleigh....................**5B 16**
Vulcan Cl. SO15: South................... 4D 28
Vulcan Rd. SO15: South 4D 28
Vyse La. SO14: South 6D 4 (2B 40)

W

Wade Hill Drove SO40: Calm........5A 18
.... (not continuous)
Wades Cres. SO16: Nur....................5B 20
Wadham Cl. SO51: Rom 1E 7
Wadhurst Gdns. SO19: South..........5A 42
Wadhurst Rd. SO30: Hed E.............5A 34
Wadmore Cl. SO45: Hythe...............2F 53
Wagtail Cl. SO50: E'leigh.................5F 15
Wainwright Gdns.
SO30: Hed E................................. 6H 25
Wakefield Ct. SO18: South 2A 32
Wakefield Rd. SO18: South 2A 32
Wakeford Ct. SO51: Rom 5B 6
Wakeford Pl. SO31: Wars................6E 49
Waldegrave Cl. SO19: South 4F 41
Waldon Gdns. SO18: W End 1B 32
Walker Gdns. SO30: Hed E..............2A 34
Walker Pl. SO31: Hamb 5F 47
Walkers Cl. SO50: Fair O 2G 17
Walker's La. Nth. SO45: Blac 5E 55
Walker's La. Sth. SO45: Blac..........5F 55
Wallace Rd. SO19: South................ 4H 41
Wallington Dr. SO53: Cha F.............5C 8
Walnut Av. SO18: S'ing.................... 4G 23
Walnut Cl. SO16: South 2D 28
Walnut Cl. SO53: Cha F 4E 9
Walnut Gro. SO16: South................ 3D 28
Walnut Way SO16: Nur.....................4B 20
Walpole La. SO31: Lwr Swan 5C 44
Walsingham Gdns.
SO18: South................................. 6H 23
Waltham Cres. SO16: South 5F 21
Walton Rd. SO19: South 1D 42
Waltons Av. SO45: Holb...................4C 54
Wangfield La. SO32: Curd 2F 35
Wansbeck Cl. SO53: Cha F............. 2D 14
Warbler Cl. SO16: South..................3F 21
Warblington Cl. SO53: Cha F...........4C 14
Warburton Cl. SO19: South 1E 43

78 A-Z Southampton

Warburton Rd. – Wilton Rd.

Warburton Rd. SO19: South 6E 33
Warden Cl. SO30: W End 2D 32
Wardle Rd. SO50: Highb 6D 10
Warlock Cl. SO19: South 2D 42
Warner Cl. SO30: Hed E............2A 34
Warner M. SO30: Botl 5E 35
Warnford Ct. SO15: South 4B 30
Warren, The SO45: Holb 3B 54
Warren Av. SO16: South 1E 29
Warren Av. SO53: Cha F............. 2G 15
Warren Cl. SO16: South...............1E 29
Warren Cl. SO53: Cha F............... 2G 15
Warren Cres. SO16: South............1E 29
Warren Gdns. SO51: Rom...............3E 7
Warren Pl. SO40: Calm 1C 26
Warrior Cl. SO53: Cha F 3D 14
Warrior Pk. Ind. Est. SO53: Cha F............................. 3D 14
Warrys Cl. SO45: Hythe 6E 53
WARSASH..6B 48
Warsash Ct. SO31: Wars 6A 48
Warsash Rd. PO14: Titch................ 1H 51
Warsash Rd. PO14: Titch C 1H 51
Warsash Rd. SO31: Loc H 6B 48
.... (not continuous)
Warsash Rd. SO31: Wars 6B 48
.... (not continuous)
Warwick Cl. SO53: Cha F 3C 14
Warwick Ho. SO14: South.................... 1H 5 (5E 31)
.... (off Kent St.)
Warwick Rd. SO15: South 1H 29
Warwick Rd. SO40: Tott 3F 27
Waterbeech Dr. SO30: Hed E........3A 34
Waterhouse La. SO15: South 4F 29
Waterhouse Way SO15: South 4F 29
Water La. SO15: South 1C 4 (6B 30)
Water La. SO40: Tott 3C 26
Water La. SO45: Dib P..................4B 52
Water La. SO50: B'stke 2C 16
Waterloo Ind. Est. SO30: Hed E... 2H 33
Waterloo Rd. SO15: South..................... 1A 4 (5G 29)
Waterloo Ter. SO15: South............5B 30
Watermans La. SO45: Dib P.........5C 52
Waters Edge SO30: Hed E 5H 33
Waterside Heritage Cen., The...... 3F 53
Waterside Rd. SO51: Rom.............3C 6
Waterside Theatre & Club 3C 54
Waterworks Rd. SO21: Ott.............1C 10
Watkin Rd. SO30: Hed E...............1B 34
Watley Cl. SO16: Nur.....................4B 20
Watson Ct. SO31: Net A................6C 42
Watson Wlk. SO40: Tott 4B 26
Watton Rd. SO45: Holb..................4C 54
Watts Cl. SO16: South 1C 28
Watt's Monument 1D 4 (6B 30)
Watts Rd. SO30: Hed E...................5A 34
Wavecrest Cl. SO40: March............2E 39
Wavell Rd. SO18: South.................4A 32
Waveney Grn. SO16: South 2C 28
Waverley Av. SO31: Net A 2C 46
Waverley Cl. SO51: Rom..................3E 7
Waverley Ct. SO31: Net A..............2C 46
Waverley Rd. SO15: South 6H 29
Wayfarer Cl. SO31: Wars 6D 48
Waylands Pl. SO30: Hed E............ 1H 43
Wayside SO31: Lwr Swan...............5B 44
Weald Cl. SO31: Loc H...................3E 49
Weardale Rd. SO53: Cha F............3F 15
Weavers Pl. SO53: Cha F................5C 8
Weavills Rd. SO50: B'stke 6F 17
Webburn Gdns. SO18: W End.......6A 24
Wedgewood Cl. SO45: Holb..........4B 54
Welbeck Av. SO17: South 1D 30
Welch Way SO16: Rown 4D 20
Welland Gdns. SO18: W End 1B 32
Welland Grn. SO16: South.............3C 28
Wellbrooke Gdns. SO53: Cha F 6C 8
Wellers Cl. SO40: Tott 4B 26
Welles Rd. SO53: Cha F..................1F 15
Wellington Av. SO18: South..........4B 32
Wellington Cl. SO45: Dib P............5B 52
Wellington Ct. SO15: South 5H 29
Wellington Ct. SO30: W End..........1C 32
Wellington Pk. SO30: Hed E 2G 33
Wellington Rd. SO18: South 1F 31
Well La. SO31: Hamb................... 5G 47
Wellowbrook Cl. SO53: Cha F 1C 14
Wellow Cl. SO18: South................4C 32
Wellow Ct. SO18: South................ 3G 31
Wellow Gdns. PO14: Titch C....... 5G 49
Wells Cl. PO15: White.................. 5G 45
Wellsmoor PO14: Titch C............ 5G 49
Wells Pl. SO50: E'leigh 5A 16
Wells Rd. SO50: E'leigh 5B 16
Wellstead Way SO30: Hed E........ 1H 33
Wembley Way SO50: Fair O..........2F 17
Wendleholme Nature Reserve.....3A 48
Wentworth Gdns. SO19: South.....4B 42
Wesley Cl. SO19: South 1D 42
Wessex Bus. Pk. SO21: Col C...... 5G 11
Wessex Cl. SO45: Blac 5F 55
Wessex Ct. SO17: South 3C 30
Wessex Ct. SO19: South 1A 42
Wessex Gdns. SO51: Rom..............5E 7
Wessex Ga. SO15: South 4A 30
Wessex La. SO18: S'ing 6F 23
WESSEX NUFFIELD HEALTH HOSPITAL 5A 10
Wessex Rd. SO18: W End 6B 24
Wessex Vale Crematorium 5H 25
Wessex Way SO21: Col C 5G 11
West Bargate SO14: South.....................4D 4 (1B 40)
West Bay Rd. SO15: South......................... 3A 4 (5E 29)
Westbourne Av. SO45: Holb 4B 54
Westbourne Cres. SO17: South....2C 30
Westbourne Mans. SO17: South 2C 30
Westbroke Gdns. SO51: Rom.........3C 6
Westbrook Cl. SO31: P Ga............1E 49
Westbrook Way SO18: S'ing 5G 23
Westbury Ct. SO30: Hed E........... 6H 33
Westbury Rd. SO15: South........... 4D 28
Westcliff M. SO19: South 2F 41
Westcot Rd. SO45: Holb 5B 54
West Ct. SO15: South 3F 29
West Dr. SO50: B'stke.................. 3D 16
WEST END 2D 32
West End Local History Mus. 2D 32
West End Rd. SO18: South 4A 32
West End Rd. SO18: W End...........4A 32
West End Rd. SO19: South 1F 43
West End Rd. SO30: W End 2D 32
West End Rd. SO31: Burs 1F 43
Westering SO51: Rom 4F 7
Westerley Cl. SO31: Wars..............6C 48
Western Av. SO15: South.............. 6D 28
WESTERN COMMUNITY HOSPITAL 2E 29
Western District Cut SO15: South................................. 4H 29
Western Esplanade SO14: South Central Sta. Bri. 2B 4 (6A 30)
Western Esplanade SO14: South Town Quay 6D 4 (2B 40)
Western Esplanade SO15: South......................4B 4 (1A 40)
Western Rd. SO30: W End 2D 32
Western Rd. SO53: Cha F.............. 4G 9
Westfield Cl. SO31: Hamb..............5E 47
Westfield Cnr. SO18: S'ing 4G 23
Westfield Cres. SO53: Cha F 3E 15
Westfield Rd. SO15: South 4E 29
Westfield Rd. SO40: Tott 3F 27
Westfield Rd. SO53: Cha F 4E 15
Westgate Hall 6D 4 (2B 40)
.... (off Westgate St.)
Westgate M. SO30: W End 2E 33
Westgate St. SO14: South...................6D 4 (2B 40)
West Hill Ct. SO15: South..........................1B 4 (6A 30)
West Horton Cl. SO50: B'stke.......6E 17
West La. SO52: N Bad 2C 12
Westmarch Ct. SO17: South...........1E 31
West Marlands Rd. SO14: South 2D 4 (6B 30)
Westminster Gdns. PO14: Titch C 4G 49
Westmorland Way SO53: Cha F........................... 1G 15
WESTON 4H 41
Weston Cl. SO19: South.............. 4H 41
WESTON COMMON 1C 42
Weston Ct. SO19: South 5H 41
Weston Cres. SO18: South 4C 32
Weston Gro. Rd. SO19: South.......3F 41
Weston La. SO16: Nur 5G 19
Weston La. SO19: South.............. 5G 41
Weston Library 4H 41
Weston Pde. SO19: South............ 5G 41
Weston Rd. SO50: E'leigh.............4A 16
Weston Sailing Club 5H 41
Westover Rd. SO16: South 3A 28
West Pk. Lodge SO17: South........2C 30
.... (off Westwood Rd.)
West Pk. Rd. SO15: South......................2C 4 (6B 30)
West Quay Retail Pk. 3B 4 (1A 40)
West Quay Rd. SO15: South Southern Rd. 2A 4 (1A 40)
West Quay Rd. SO15: South W. Quay Rd. Ind. Est. 2A 40
West Quay Rd. Ind. Est. SO15: South 5B 4 (2A 40)
Westridge Ct. SO17: South......... 2D 30
Westridge Rd. SO17: South 2D 30
West Rd. SO19: South 3G 41
West Rd. SO30: Hed E 5F 33
West Rd. SO45: Dib P....................5B 52
West Rd. SO45: Hard 6H 53
Westrow Gdns. SO15: South 4A 30
Westrow Rd. SO15: South 4A 30
West St. SO14: South 5D 4 (2B 40)
West St. SO45: Hythe.....................2C 52
Westward Rd. SO30: Hed E...........3A 34
West (Watts) Pk. 1D 4 (6B 30)
Westways Cl. SO16: Nur 4B 20
Westwood Ct. SO17: South 2C 30
Westwood Ct. SO30: W End 2D 32
Westwood Ct. SO40: Tott 1E 27
Westwood Gdns. SO53: Cha F 6G 9
Westwood Mans. SO17: South.....2C 30
WESTWOOD PARK.........................2C 30
Westwood Rd. SO17: South 3B 30
Westwood Rd. SO31: Net A..........6B 42
Westwood Woodland Pk...............5A 42
Wetherby Ct. SO40: Tott...............3C 26
Wetherby Gdns. SO40: Tott...........3C 26
Weybridge Cl. SO31: Sar G.......... 1D 48
Whalesmead Cl. SO50: B'stke...... 6E 17
Whalesmead Rd. SO50: B'stke..... 6E 17
Wharf Rd. SO19: South..................2F 41
Wharncliffe Ho. SO19: South.........2F 41
Wharncliffe Rd. SO19: South 2F 41
Whartons Cl. SO40: A'hst 2C 36
Whartons La. SO40: A'hst 1C 36
Wheat Cl. SO53: Cha F 1B 14
Wheatcroft Dr. SO18: South 2B 32
Wheatlands PO14: Titch C............ 3G 49
Wheatsheaf Ct. SO30: Hed E......... 5H 33
Wheelers Mdw. SO31: Old N 4E 43
Wheelers Wlk. SO45: Blac.............5F 55
Wheelhouse Pk. Cvn. Pk. SO52: N Bad 4B 8
Whernside Cl. SO16: South 3D 28
Whinchat Cl. SO16: South 3F 21
Whinfield Rd. SO45: Dib P.............5C 52
Whistler Cl. SO19: South................2C 42
Whistler Rd. SO19: South..............2C 42
Whitchurch Ct. SO19: South 2H 41
Whitcombe Cl. SO40: Tott 4E 27
Whitebeam Cl. SO21: Col C 5G 11
Whitebeam Rd. SO30: Hed E.........5B 34
Whitebeam Way SO52: N Bad.......2E 13
Whitecroft SO45: Hythe.................4E 53
Whitefield Rd. SO45: Holb 5B 54
White Harmony Acres Ind. Est. SO30: W End 4E 25
White Hart Rd. SO50: Fair O..........2F 17
Whitehaven Home Pk. SO45: Blac 5E 55
White Heather Ct. SO45: Hythe.....1E 53
Whitehill Cl. SO18: South 3C 32
Whitehouse Gdns. SO15: South ...5E 29
Whitelaw Rd. SO15: South 4F 29
WHITELEY..5G 45
WHITELEY FARM RDBT. 4H 45
Whiteley La. SO31: Burr.................3F 45
Whiteley Way PO15: White.......... 4H 45
WHITENAP 6F 7
Whitenap Cl. SO51: Rom 5E 7
Whitenap La. SO51: Rom 5E 7
White Rd. SO50: B'stke 3D 16
Whites La. SO45: F'ley 2H 55
White's Rd. SO19: South 6A 32
White Star Pl. SO14: South......................5G 5 (2D 40)
White Star Way SO14: South........3C 40
Whitestone Cl. SO16: South 3D 28
Whites Way SO30: Hed E.............. 1H 33
Whitewater Ri. SO45: Dib P 4C 52
Whithedwood Av. SO15: South ... 3H 29
Whittle Av. PO15: Seg.................. 2G 49
Whitwell SO31: Net A...................6C 42
Whitworth Ct. SO18: South 3F 31
Whitworth Cres. SO18: South 3F 31
Whitworth Rd. SO18: South 3F 31
Whyte Cl. SO45: Holb 5B 54
Whyteways SO50: E'leigh...............3A 16
Wicket, The SO45: Hythe...............4C 52
Wickham Ct. SO40: Tott.................4E 27
Wickham Ho. SO17: South 2C 30
Wickham Rd. SO32: Curd............ 4G 35
Wicklow Dr. SO53: Cha F 2C 14
Widecombe Dr. SO45: Hythe 3C 52
Wide La. SO18: S'ing 4G 23
Wide La. SO18: S'ton A................. 4G 23
Wide La. SO50: E'leigh 2H 23
Wide Lane Sports Complex 2H 23
Widgeon Cl. SO16: South 3F 21
Wightway M. SO31: Wars..............6A 48
Wild Arum Way SO53: Cha F.........2B 14
Wildburn Cl. SO40: Calm...............1B 26
Wild Cherry Way SO53: Cha F......1C 14
Wilde Cl. SO40: Tott 4C 26
WILDERN 3A 34
Wildern Cl. SO31: Loc H 4D 48
Wildern Ct. SO30: Hed E............... 3H 33
Wilderness Hgts. SO18: W End 2C 32
Wildern La. SO30: Hed E 3A 34
Wildern Leisure Cen. 4A 34
Wildground La. SO45: Hythe 5E 53
Wild Rose Cres. SO31: Loc H 5C 48
Wildwood Cl. PO14: Titch C.......... 1H 51
Wilkins Rd. SO30: Hed E 2A 34
Wilks Cl. SO16: Nur........................4A 20
William Ho. SO16: South 4E 21
William Macleod Way SO16: South....................................2E 29
William Panter Ct. SO50: E'leigh...........................5A 16
Williams Cl. SO45: Holb.................5C 54
William St. SO14: South 6E 31
Willis Av. SO52: N Bad...................3F 13
Willis Rd. SO16: S'ing.....................4F 23
Willment Marine & Bus. Pk. SO19: South 1F 41
Willments Ind. Est. SO19: South......................................2E 41
Willow Cl. SO30: Hed E 5B 34
Willow Cl. SO30: W End.................1E 33
Willow Ct. SO16: South 6E 21
Willow Dr. SO40: March............... 5D 38
Willow Gdns. SO52: N Bad 2C 12
Willow Grn. SO21: Col C 5G 11
Willow Gro. SO50: Fair O 2G 17
Willow Herb Cl. SO31: Loc H.........5C 48
Willow Mead SO30: Hed E............. 3H 33
Willows, The PO14: Titch C 3G 49
Willows, The SO30: W End 1E 33
Willows, The SO53: Cha F 4E 15
Willow Tree Wlk. SO19: South......2B 42
Wilmer Rd. SO50: E'leigh 5A 16
Wilmington Cl. SO18: South......... 6H 23
Wilmot Cl. SO50: B'stke 2E 17
Wilroy Gdns. SO16: South 1D 28
Wilson St. SO14: South 1H 5 (6E 31)
Wilton Av. SO15: South..................5A 30
Wilton Ct. SO15: South 3H 29
Wilton Cres. SO15: South 2H 29
Wilton Gdns. SO15: South 2H 29
Wilton Mnr. SO15: South 5B 30
.... (off Wilton Av.)
Wilton Rd. SO15: South................ 1G 29

Published by Geographers' A-Z Map Company Limited
An imprint of HarperCollins Publishers
Westerhill Road
Bishopbriggs
Glasgow
G64 2QT

www.az.co.uk
a-z.maps@harpercollins.co.uk

HarperCollinsPublishers
Macken House, 39/40 Mayor Street Upper, Dublin 1, D01 C9W8, Ireland

9th edition 2021

© Collins Bartholomew Ltd 2021

This product uses map data licenced from Ordnance Survey
© Crown copyright and database rights 2020 OS 100018598

AZ, A-Z and AtoZ are registered trademarks of Geographers' A-Z Map Company Limited